CAMBRIDGE LIBRARY COLLECTION

Books of enduring scholarly value

History

The books reissued in this series include accounts of historical events and movements by eye-witnesses and contemporaries, as well as landmark studies that assembled significant source materials or developed new historiographical methods. The series includes work in social, political and military history on a wide range of periods and regions, giving modern scholars ready access to influential publications of the past.

Greater Rome and Greater Britain

In later Victorian England, although classical literature had long dominated education, Roman history and politics became popular areas of study, particularly after Queen Victoria became Empress of India in 1877. Many writers on colonialism drew parallels between the Roman and British Empires, but Sir Charles Lucas's book, first published in 1912, went further in its analysis. He stresses that the causes of an empire's growth and strength are numerous, and that geography and technological development are particularly important. Like writers such as Froude, he attempts to forecast the future development of the British Empire. He also points out differences between the two empires. Roman expansion was not accompanied by widespread emigration, in the way that British colonists settled North America and Australasia, for example. British India, manifesting the military and economic domination of a much larger subject people by a tiny administrative class, bore more resemblance to Roman imperialism.

T0370683

Cambridge University Press has long been a pioneer in the reissuing of out-of-print titles from its own backlist, producing digital reprints of books that are still sought after by scholars and students but could not be reprinted economically using traditional technology. The Cambridge Library Collection extends this activity to a wider range of books which are still of importance to researchers and professionals, either for the source material they contain, or as landmarks in the history of their academic discipline.

Drawing from the world-renowned collections in the Cambridge University Library, and guided by the advice of experts in each subject area, Cambridge University Press is using state-of-the-art scanning machines in its own Printing House to capture the content of each book selected for inclusion. The files are processed to give a consistently clear, crisp image, and the books finished to the high quality standard for which the Press is recognised around the world. The latest print-on-demand technology ensures that the books will remain available indefinitely, and that orders for single or multiple copies can quickly be supplied.

The Cambridge Library Collection will bring back to life books of enduring scholarly value (including out-of-copyright works originally issued by other publishers) across a wide range of disciplines in the humanities and social sciences and in science and technology.

Greater Rome
and Greater Britain

SIR CHARLES PRESTWOOD LUCAS

CAMBRIDGE
UNIVERSITY PRESS

CAMBRIDGE UNIVERSITY PRESS

Cambridge, New York, Melbourne, Madrid, Cape Town, Singapore,
São Paolo, Delhi, Dubai, Tokyo, Mexico City

Published in the United States of America by Cambridge University Press, New York

www.cambridge.org
Information on this title: www.cambridge.org/9781108024013

© in this compilation Cambridge University Press 2010

This edition first published 1912
This digitally printed version 2010

ISBN 978-1-108-02401-3 Paperback

GREATER ROME
AND
GREATER BRITAIN

HENRY FROWDE, M.A.
PUBLISHER TO THE UNIVERSITY OF OXFORD
LONDON, EDINBURGH, NEW YORK, TORONTO
MELBOURNE AND BOMBAY

GREATER ROME

AND

GREATER BRITAIN

BY

SIR C. P. LUCAS

K.C.B., K.C.M.G.

OXFORD

AT THE CLARENDON PRESS

1912

PREFACE

THIS book is intended to illustrate, by comparison with the Roman Empire, some features of the British Empire as they have appeared to me.

I have to thank Mr. P. E. Matheson, Fellow of New College, for some valuable suggestions and corrections.

C. P. L.

November, 1912.

CONTENTS

CHAPTER I

ROMAN TERMS

WHEN we speak of British lands and peoples beyond the seas, and of their relation to the Motherland, we nearly always use words which are of Roman origin. *Colony, dependency, plantation, province, state, possession, dominion, empire,* all directly or indirectly come from the Romans. One Saxon word, *settle* with its derivatives, holds a prominent place in reference to the beginnings of colonies; and, in taking the name of *commonwealth,* Australia has in part borrowed from the Saxons. But all or nearly all the terms which indicate the political status of Greater Britain and its component parts are a legacy from Rome.

What did the Romans mean by their terms, and what do we mean by them? It will be enough to take the four words, *colony, province, dominion,* and *empire,* leaving out *dependency, plantation,* and *state,* and only noting of *possession* that *possessio* in Roman law indicated actual occupation with intent to retain —for small populations in large lands a useful and suggestive word, and that by the Interpretation Act of 1889 'the expression British possession shall mean any part of Her Majesty's dominions exclusive of the United Kingdom'.

B

In its etymology the Roman word *colonia* was equivalent to *plantation*. The root-meaning of the word was cultivation of the land, and in the later Roman Empire the *coloni* were a class of small-holders, free men but bound to the soil.[1] Starting from this root-meaning, *colonia* like *plantation* came to indicate in some sort a colony. But, as compared with the English word *colony* in its ordinary sense, the Roman word *colonia* implied rather the body of men and women who went out to settle than the place in which they settled; and, so far as place was indicated, it was a town rather than a country, and not so much a new town or settle-ment as an existing community, into which Roman citizens were drafted, and where in many cases they were allotted lands which had already been in use and of which the former holders were dis-possessed. Thus the word *colonia* implied removal of citizens from an old home to a new, and the derivation of the word indicated agricultural settle-ment. But otherwise there was no similarity between a Roman *colonia* and a British *colony*. There was no dispersion of Romans over a new and wide area, no squatting, no winning of back-wood, prairie, or bush. The Roman *colonia* more often than not contained the element of military occupation. It was rather a permanently established garrison of Romans in the midst of a conquered

---

[1] For the coloni see Pelham's *Essays on Roman History* (1911), chap. xiii, pp. 275, &c., *The Imperial Domains and the Colonate.*

community than a colony or settlement in the modern sense.

The etymology of the word *provincia* has always been disputed. If the old account of it holds good, the word implied conquest. But its original meaning was not geographical, for the word implied a charge of business, the duties allotted to one Roman official or another. *Provincia*, however, soon came to be applied to the area within which those duties were performed, and to denote this or that district of the Roman Empire outside Italy. 'Amongst the Romans it was used for a country without the limits of Italy, gained to their subjection by conquest.'[1] The Roman Empire was almost entirely the result of conquest, and in no sense the outcome of discovery and settlement. Its component parts were dependencies, and those dependencies outside Italy were called *provinciae*.

Dominium in Roman law denoted ownership in its fullest sense ; the sum total of rights over property, including slaves. It implied despotism pure and simple. This despotism was openly avowed, when Diocletian took the title of *dominus*, which earlier Roman emperors had rejected. But the word *dominium* was never given, as the English word *dominion* has been given, and as *provincia* was given, a geographical meaning. It always indicated purely personal rights.

---

[1] Stokes, *Constitution of the British Colonies in North America and the West Indies*, 1783, chap. i, p. 2.

Imperium denoted the full authority of the State entrusted to an individual. It included all the powers of the State, military, administrative, and judicial, and was limited only by the time for which, and the area within which, those powers could be exercised. The word, therefore, had by no means a purely military connotation, though armed force was never far from Roman hands or Roman minds. The pages of the classics, especially those of post-Augustan writers, show that *imperium*, like *provincia*, acquired a geographical as well as a personal meaning, and was often used as equivalent to our English word *empire*.

The English word *colony*, like the Latin word *colonia*, originally indicated the people who emigrated rather than the place to which they emigrated. The place to which they emigrated was rather known as a *plantation*, and the first beginning of a Colonial Office was a Committee of the Privy Council for the Plantations. 'In strict propriety of speech, colony denotes the people emigrated, and plantation the place in which they are settled.'[1] The word, however, soon came to have a territorial meaning, and the Interpretation Act of 1889 defines a colony as 'any part of Her Majesty's dominions, exclusive of the British islands and of British India'. The modern history of the term *colony* is interesting. Writing in 1783, Stokes tells us that 'For some time before the Civil War broke

[1] Stokes, p. 2.

out in America, the popular leaders there affected
to call the Provincial Establishments, or King's
Governments on the continent, colonies, instead
of provinces, from an opinion they had conceived,
that the word province meant a conquered country'.[1]
In other words, the Americans were still thinking
of *colony* in the sense of the people rather than the
land, and did not wish its meaning to be confounded
with that of *dependency*. But the term *colony* was
taken to include both colonies proper and dependencies, which were the result of conquest rather
than of settlement; and the latest phase is that
the colonies proper have rejected the word *colony*
as implying youth, tutelage, and dependence, and,
with the exception of Newfoundland, have adopted
or been given the title of *dominions*, leaving *colonies*
to indicate the Crown Colonies or semi-Crown
Colonies, which are in fact dependencies rather
than colonies in the true sense.

The term *province*, as has been seen, was, in the
earlier days of North American colonization, often
applied to those of the colonies now included in the
United States of America which had governors
appointed by the Crown, whereas 'a plantation,
in which the governor was elected by the inhabitants, was usually called a colony, as the colony of
Connecticut'; but the word has, as a rule, been
used without any very specific signification, with
the exception that it has never been 'applied to an

[1] Stokes, p. 3.

insular government '.[1] In Canada *province* is
roughly equivalent to *state* in Australia. In other
words it means one or other of the units which
form the confederation or Dominion ; and, inasmuch
as the units which make up the Dominion of Canada
are or were more restricted in their powers than
those of which the Commonwealth of Australia
is composed, the term *province* may be said to
imply less freedom than the term *state*, although
this meaning or implication is, perhaps, more a
matter of accident than a suggestion of the original
derivation of the Roman *provincia.*

Dominion, used geographically, may be said to
have a double sense. We speak of the whole
British Empire as the King's Dominions, the lands
which own His Majesty as their lord and master.
It is also used in these latter days to denote the
groups of self-governing colonies, which seems to
involve the paradox that the name which of all
others most implies despotism has been given to
the most independent parts of the Empire. The
origin of the paradox is in Canada. The founders
of Canadian confederation, or one of them, Sir John
Macdonald, wished to christen the new confederation the Kingdom of Canada ; and, when that term
was rejected as not being in harmony with American
surroundings, the name of *dominion* was chosen,
which seemed nearest akin to Kingdom, and which
had previously been given to the colony of Virginia,

[1] Stokes, p. 3.

styled the 'Old Dominion'.[1] Accordingly the British
North America Act of 1867 prescribed that the
confederating provinces 'shall form and be one
Dominion under the name of Canada'. The application of the term *dominion* to a group of self-
governing colonies may be defended as follows.
The term implies a sovereign lord, and brings
the territory in question into direct relation to
the sovereign lord. It implies subordination to the
Crown, but to the Crown alone, and thereby it
eliminates subordination to any one or anything
else. Thus it may be construed as a declaration that
the self-governing territory is not subordinate to the
United Kingdom, but equally with the United Kingdom subordinate to the sovereign lord of both. In
other words it may be held to imply unity of head-
ship, and equality of partners under the one head.

It will be noted that *dominion* in modern parlance
has more especially come to be used as the name
for a confederation of self-governing colonies, that it
grew up side by side with the confederation movement in North America and Australasia. But New
Zealand, though originally the result of confederation, was, by Royal Proclamation of 1907, formally
given the title of *dominion*, long after it had been

---

[1] When King Charles I was executed, the governor of Virginia
proclaimed Charles II King of England, Scotland, Ireland, and
Virginia, and for a time the arms of Virginia were quartered with
those of England, Scotland, and Ireland. Hence the title ' The Old
Dominions' arose. Virginia was in fact the first Dominion in the
sense in which the term dominion is now used in the British Empire.

unified, and without any further change in its status or composition. Newfoundland, on the other hand, though it takes rank among the self-governing Dominions, still keeps, as a single entity, the name of colony, and is not known as the Dominion of Newfoundland. It is the oldest British colony, and adheres to the name.

Lastly, the term *empire* is used to include the whole of the British possessions at home and abroad. It is a term which has aroused much prejudice, because it has come to imply military rule to a greater extent than the Roman word *imperium*, from which it is derived. The King is Emperor of India, but of no other part of his dominions; and when the title of Empress of India was first conferred upon Queen Victoria, there were some in Parliament who raised their voices against it. Those who object to the use of the word *empire* forget that in past times it was valuable to England, as implying her independence of foreign rulers and not her possession of foreign dependencies. 'The meaning, therefore, of the Legislature, when it uses these terms of Empire and Imperial, and applies them to the realm and Crown of England, is only to assert that our King is equally sovereign and independent within these his dominions, as any emperor is in his empire.'[1] In this sense a statute

[1] Blackstone's *Commentaries*, 1800 ed., Bk. I, cap. 7, vol. i, p. 242. The statute referred to is 24 Henry VIII, cap. 12. See the *Oxford English Dictionary*, s.v.

of Henry VIII declares that 'This realme of England is an Empire'. Even taking *empire* in its modern and popular sense, there is no other single word which so well covers the *immensum imperii corpus*; it is strictly accurate, as applied to one half of the British possessions; and, if it is less appropriate, as applied to the other half, it at least serves to remind us of the complex nature of Greater Britain, and of the historical truth that the present system is not the result of peaceful growth alone, but of peace maintained by adequate protection.

Having thus illustrated the debt which we owe to the Romans for our terminology in regard to the British possessions overseas and their relations to Great Britain, it is proposed in the following pages to examine some of the leading features of the British Empire, and to compare and contrast them with the characteristics of the Roman Empire, which was the greatest political system of the ancient world.

CHAPTER II

SPACE

CLIMATE, race, many other factors contribute to the actual present and the coming future of the British Empire; but there is one element in it which, in the sense in which it will be noticed in this chapter, does not often receive as much notice as it deserves. That element is space. What part has space played, and what part is it still playing, in the moulding of the Empire? The question is important in regard to that half of the Empire which contains the self-governing Dominions. If we consider the relations of those Dominions to the United Kingdom, one aspect of the question, as it stands at the present day, is that we have large areas with small populations linked to a small area with a large population.

Assuming for the sake of the argument two countries; one small, the other large; one full, the other empty; and assuming further that all the population of the empty land comes from the well filled small area, then, even if the climate, soil, and general conditions of the two countries are much the same, the mere fact that men and women who have previously lived closely packed together

are transplanted into great spaces, and that their
children are born and bred in great spaces, will
produce a somewhat different type of people. The
great spaces of the British Empire already have
had much and will have more to say to its history.

This element of space does not appear to have
had any very appreciable effect in the Roman
Empire. We are not now considering the total
area of that Empire as compared with the British
Empire, nor the size of any one province as compared with one of the British overseas Dominions.
We are considering the nature of the settlement
in either case. A large number of Roman men
and Roman families emigrated to and settled in
the Provinces; their children grew up amid new
surroundings and varied according to the surroundings; but their lives, characters, and physique do
not seem to have been influenced by space to the
same extent as those of British emigrants to the
self-governing Dominions. The tradition, instinct,
and policy of the Romans was, so far as they
colonized with their own citizens, rather to found
new or to reinforce old town communities than to
settle loosely large areas of countryside; and, wide
as was the field in which Roman colonies were
planted, it consisted entirely of conquered lands,
the natives of which were comparatively numerous
and strong, so that, especially as they lived in days
when fire-arms had not been invented, even if the
Romans had wished to disperse in their settlement, it

would not have been safe for them to do so. 'A purely
rural region, where the people live in villages only,
was contrary to Roman interests and traditions.'[1]
This does not mean that there was no country life
among the Romans in the provinces. There was
country life there, as in Italy, as is shown by Roman
villas unearthed on English soil; and the State-
planted colonies seem in all or most of the provinces
to have been supplemented by groups of Roman or
Italian traders and farmers, who made their homes
among the provincials outside as well as inside
existing towns. But the broad fact remains that
in Adam Smith's words the Roman colonies 'were
all established in conquered provinces, which, in
most cases, had been fully inhabited before'[2]; that
therefore the Roman Empire was a sphere of rule
rather than a sphere of settlement; that the leading
feature of Roman colonization was that it consisted
in the main of towns and military stations on great
highways; and that a large proportion of Roman
settlers were soldiers accustomed, as soldiers and
ex-soldiers always are, to live in company. Thus
it appears that Roman colonization and modern
British colonization differed wholly in kind, and
that it was not characteristic of Roman colonization
to make new homes in large spaces.

[1] *Rome*, in the Home University Library Series, by W. Warde
Fowler, p. 214.
[2] *Wealth of Nations*, chap. vii, pt. ii: Causes of the prosperity of
New Colonies.

The self-governing Dominions of the British Empire include in their populations other races than the British. This element of space has, perhaps more than any other, made the Dutch race in South Africa what it is at the present day. At home, in the Netherlands, the Dutch lived close together in a very small area; and, as their land was straitened and confined, Dutch enterprise found its outlet on the sea. The Dutch went to South Africa, the Netherlands East India Company founded a trading-station at the Cape, a few Dutch settlers made their permanent homes in South Africa, some few of them became Boers or farmers, and very gradually settlement straggled inland. Then political causes made for dispersion. Even before the English took the Cape, the Dutch farmers of Graaf Reinet were up in arms against the restrictive rule of the Netherlands East India Company, while, after the Cape became a British possession, the Great Trek took place, and South African Dutchmen went out more and more into space, though it was not empty space, but wilderness tenanted by wild men and wild beasts. Thus, while the story of the Dutch in Holland was a story of towns and ships and sea, the story of the Dutch in South Africa was one of pastoral and hunting life, from which the towns and the sea were eliminated, and where wagons took the place of ships. Great spaces have made the Boers, alike in character and in physique, a distinct type of Dutchmen.

The case of the French in Canada was not parallel
to that of the Dutch in South Africa. France is
a much more spacious land than Holland, and on
the other hand, French colonization in Canada was
so directed and regulated by the government as to
keep French settlement continuous on seigniories
along the banks of the St. Lawrence, and more
especially at or near the three centres of Quebec,
Three Rivers, and Montreal. 'The inhabitants of
French origin are chiefly distributed along the
banks of the St. Lawrence, as far up as Montreal.
The land adjacent to this magnificent river exhibits
the appearance of a continuous line of villages—a
military mode of settlement.'[1] The French colonization of Canada had in it a touch of Roman settlement. It was in its essence largely military colonization. It was despotically arranged, organized, and
held together, in order to keep the land against
notable Indian fighters with hostile British colonies
behind them. It is true that there were outlying
forts and fur stations further west; and, as against
the habitants attached to the soil on the seigniories,
there grew up a race of wandering voyageurs and
coureurs de bois, who were always on the move.
But, though explorers and hunters and traders were
constantly in evidence, going into and coming back
from the wilds, there was no wholesale trekking or
dispersion of the population far inland. Moreover,

[1] From Appendix C to *Lord Durham's Report*, 1912 ed., vol. iii,
p. 142.

as on the one hand the sea did not dominate the homeland of France and its people to the same extent as it dominated the Netherlands and the Dutch, so, on the other hand, the Province of Quebec was very far from being an inland home for the French, such as South Africa was for the Dutch. Living on the St. Lawrence, the French in Canada always kept in touch with the sea. In other words, widely different as Canada was from France, the French settlers in Canada were not transported into such wholly different surroundings as was the case with the Dutch in South Africa; and, from the nature and the design of French-Canadian settlement, great spaces did not mould the character of the French-Canadians, as they moulded the character of the Boers in South Africa. It was when in later times the prairies were reached, and the North-West was opened for British rather than for French colonists, that space began to tell.

The most purely British of the self-governing Dominions are Newfoundland, Australia, and New Zealand; and of all parts of the British Empire it is in Australia that the effect of space has been most marked. Here, more than anywhere else, the people have been moulded by what the Australian poet has called 'the never ending plains'. At the same time there is this curious feature in Australian settlement, that a very large proportion of the scanty population of Australia is congregated in towns. Some 35 per cent. of the total population is in the six capital cities, all of which are on or near the sea, and more than half the population is in towns of over 5,000 inhabitants. Melbourne and Adelaide account for between 40 and 50 per cent. of the population of Victoria and South Australia respectively. But, over and above the fact that the cities and towns are spread over a very much larger area of ground than is the case in the United Kingdom, it is the country rather than the town which has given and is giving its distinctive character to the coming Australian nation. It is the bush rather than the sea which calls to the Australian, and the future is being fashioned by the back blocks with their widely dispersed and much isolated stations. Those who wish to account for any difference between the English in the United Kingdom and the English in Australia must set it down largely to the influence of space, and those who want to find the exact antipodes to Roman colonization will find it in the story of Australia. Merivale writes that ' the latest conquests of Rome annexed the backwoods of Gaul and Germany in great masses ', but he adds that ' even here the colonization of the Romans, and even the occupation of the natives, was confined to certain narrow tracks of internal communication '.[1] What did not exist in the Roman Empire and what does exist in the British Empire is a steady stream of citizens going out from the

[1] *History of the Romans under the Empire*, 1865 ed., vol. iv, chap. xxxix, pp. 389-90.

homeland into what the Romans would have called the provinces, and there making their new homes on their own lines, scattered and isolated in great spaces.

This element of space makes for diversity. There is infinite diversity in the British Empire. Even in that part of it which is comprised in the self-governing Dominions, there is the greatest variety of race, language and so forth. In the present connexion we are dealing only with diversity as the result of space, and the question arises, How far is the Empire likely to lose or to gain in unity and strength from the fact that great spaces tend to produce different types of the same race?

At first sight it would seem that the more uniform in type communities are, the more likely they are to cohere. But, judging from private as well as from national life, it may be questioned whether cohesion is not more likely to arise from supplementing than from duplicating. Within limits there is less probability of friction between those who have points of difference than between those who are in all respects the same. In the latter case there is at best wearisome iteration, in the former case one supplies what the other wants. We may find an analogy in the geography of Australia. Federation or unification of Australia might well have been an easier matter, if the States which make up the Commonwealth had differed more in kind from each other, if they had felt more need of

one another on the ground that each one obviously
contributed to the whole what the others had not,
instead of being to a very large extent uniform and
therefore repeating one another, differing in quantity
rather than in quality. Similarly it may fairly be
argued that the Empire as a whole gains from the
fact that the British race within it, while funda-
mentally the same, develops in different surroundings different characteristics. A concrete illustration
might be found in the late South African war, which
was a war in great spaces, and in which the overseas contingents, mounted men habituated to great
spaces, admirably supplemented the regular troops
from home.

Now, although Canada includes the Rocky Mountains and the Selkirks, New Zealand the New
Zealand Alps, while fine mountains are also to be
found in Australia and South Africa, yet the great
spaces of the self-governing Dominions are in the
main not mountain regions, but plains and plateaux.
In these Dominions, therefore, space may be said to
work its full will upon the incoming British race.
On the effects which this cause produces it would
be misleading to attempt to generalize, because the
conditions of one Dominion differ widely from those
of another, and many other elements than space,
among them notably climate, contribute to the net
result. But if we compare the Australian Englishman, for example, with the home grown product,
we find in the former what may be called the open-

air characteristics of the Englishman quickened and intensified, and may fairly attribute this result to the influence, direct or indirect, of the bush. We find in the Australian a greater degree, or at any rate more outward signs, of freedom and equality, greater absence of reserve, greater impatience of restraint and discipline, stronger instinct of race kinship and more spontaneous welcome and hospitality. He is an Englishman who has grown at will with ample elbow room and has not been trimmed and pruned in a confined area and an ordered place. He contributes to the British Empire a citizen of British race but of somewhat different type from the resident in the United Kingdom. It cannot be doubted that this different type makes for increased vitality of the Empire.

The United Kingdom, being small and thickly peopled, overflows into the spaces of the Dominions, and many years must pass before these spaces are filled. There is no appreciable counter current. Not a few individuals, it is true, from time to time return or come from the Dominions to the Motherland ; South African millionaires bring back their gold, Canadians find seats in the House of Commons, Rhodes scholars go to Oxford ; but the number all told is not large ; and, so far as England has received any lasting impress from overseas Englishmen, it has perhaps come mainly from those who have done their life's work in the tropical half of the Empire, and who have always retained actual or potential

homes in England, with full *animus revertendi.*
Men of the type of retired Indian civil servants,
trained in administration, have probably left more
mark on life and thought in England than is usually
recognized, while the self-governing Dominions have,
from the nature of the case, so far been rather
engaged in receiving Englishmen and assimilating
them to their great spaces than in contributing from
their own citizens to the population of the United
Kingdom.   This means that England is at present
leavening the Dominions more than the Dominions
are leavening England, but on the other hand, that
the proportion of Englishmen of the type which
great spaces produce is constantly increasing.   There
must in the course of history come a time when
the lands will be filled and space will cease to tell,
but by that time by far the larger number of citizens
of British race within the Empire, if the Empire
holds together, will be of the type which space has
dictated.   Therefore, not only in order to appreciate
present differences, but also in order to estimate
the future, it is well to give some thought to space
as one of the factors which is moulding the British
Empire, and which was wanting in the Roman
Empire.

CHAPTER III

YOUTH

THE connexion of England with India is that of a comparatively modern community of Western type with Old World systems and civilization of wholly different origin. The connexion of England with the self-governing Dominions is that of a comparatively old community with young nations in the making, on similar lines to, and of more or less the same material as, the older people. Still confining ourselves for the moment to the latter case, the relations between the self-governing Dominions and the Mother Country, and having considered the effect of space, let us consider in a sense the effect of time, and regard the relations in question as relations between youth and age.

Here again there is no analogy to be found in the Roman Empire. The Romans ruled and left their mark upon a conquered world, just as we rule and are leaving our mark upon India. They gave organization, laws, institutions, language, roads, and buildings, but they did not give birth to and rear from subordination to equality young peoples of their own Roman race. So far as they colonized, they colonized, as has been seen, to a large extent in towns, and these towns had no separate political existence. They were little off-shoots of Rome and garrisons of Romans ; one and another had municipal privileges ; but they were never intended to be, and never were, the beginnings of new peoples. A nearer approach to British colonization is to be found in the history of Greece than in that of Rome. The Greek cities were in the fullest sense parents of other Greek cities overseas ; but the connexion between the child and the parent was one of sentiment only, the two were entirely independent of one another, the colony as often as not grew to full strength as soon as the mother city, and we look in vain to Greece for a political system including within it states bearing such relations to each other as exist between the self-governing Dominions and the United Kingdom. There is, in fact, no parallel to it in the history of the world. The gradual growth of younger British peoples within and not without the Empire, the maintenance of the connexion between the young and the old, coupled with the continuous development from terms of subordination to terms of practical independence, is peculiar to the British race.

Without attempting here to analyse the causes which have led to existing conditions, or discussing how far the lessons learnt from the American War of Independence and its outcome affected the subsequent course of British colonial history, we can take facts as we find them, and those facts are that one-half of the British Empire consists of an old people and young peoples linked together on terms of growing equality.

Peoples are relatively old and young, only so far as they form separate entities. Rome had older buildings and associations than a Roman colony in Gaul or Britain possessed. But a Roman colony was not a people or the nucleus of a people, for it had no political individuality apart from Rome. The self-governing Dominions of the British Empire, on the other hand, in their relation to the Mother Country, are distinct and separate entities, although both they and the Mother Country are parts of one Empire and under one sovereign. They are related as the older and younger members of a family ; and this old and very simple analogy of the family supplies the only terms which make the present position as between the Mother Country and the Dominions intelligible.

The Roman State started with the family, and the Roman Empire reproduced the Roman family in so far as the Roman family, like the Roman Empire, was under a despotism, the *patria potestas*. The British family is on a different model.

In a well ordered British family the sons, while they are children, are governed, protected, trained, and paid for, but always with the direct object of making them, when they come to man's estate, self-dependent and able to stand on their own footing. When grown up, they are helped with capital, if the father has capital, to start

them in life ; and if there is a family firm, they
are given their articles and eventually taken into
partnership. They are not expected to pass their
lives under the same roof as their parents and in
the same household, but to make and be masters
of their own separate homes, to create new ties and
bring a new strain into the family, of which they
none the less remain strong, active, and attached
members. For the purpose of the analogy, it will be
noted that the object of the father, if he is a wise,
right-minded man, and the outcome of his family
policy, is to promote independence but not complete
separation, and by means of independence, not in
spite of independence, to retain the life-long allegiance and affection of the children. It will be noted
too that, in normal circumstances and in the course
of nature, the giving is almost wholly on the part
of the father, who finds his *quid pro quo* in the
affection of the children and the knowledge that
they recognize, and if need were to come, would be
prepared to make good what they owe to him.

This is a sketch of the relations within what we
have called a well-ordered family. The key of the
whole is continuous adjustment between youth and
age, constant concession from the old to the young
in the direction of greater freedom, carrying on the
son from tutelage to free agency, transforming the
parent from a despot into at most a predominant
partner, the whole evolution being sound, reason-
able, and according to nature. Failures come and

rifts in the family circle from unduly prolonging the parental despotism, in other words from not recognizing in time what is the inevitable result of time, or from cutting the son adrift at too early an age, in other words from being premature and trying to forestall time.

It is true that the analogy between individuals and communities fails in that communities do not die like the individual men and women of which they are composed. But, just as the father's aim is to rear children who will carry on his name and perpetuate his work, so it lies with fruitful colonizing peoples to rear communities which, even if the worst were to befall, will in some sort uphold the race and the name. This sentiment is expressed in fine language in Lord Durham's Report on Canada. 'Our first duty', he wrote, 'is to secure the well-being of our colonial countrymen; and if in the hidden decrees of that wisdom by which the world is ruled, it is written that these countries are not for ever to remain portions of the Empire, we owe it to our honour to take good care that, when they separate from us, they should not be the only countries on the American continent in which the Anglo-Saxon race shall be found unfit to govern itself.' [1]

But Lord Durham did not contemplate dissolution of the Empire. He contemplated continued life for it and growing strength, by giving greater freedom

[1] 1912 ed., vol. ii, p. 310.

to communities which had outgrown the stage of childhood. It has been said above that in families friction causing or tending to separation arises either from not relaxing authority and making concessions when the time for concessions is due, or from insisting upon the son fending for himself entirely before he is entirely fitted to do so. In the history of the relations between England and the self-governing Dominions, usually but not always at different times and in different cases, the Mother Country has laid herself open to two charges diametrically opposed to each other, the first being the charge of interference, the second the charge of indifference. At the time when Lord Durham wrote, and for the better part of twenty years afterwards, government from Downing Street was the bugbear of the younger peoples of the Empire, and their constant complaint was that they were not allowed to manage their own affairs in their own way without continual interference from home. Then, when responsible government had been granted first to one colony and then to another, although from time to time complaints of interference were still made, the more general feeling was that the Mother Country and its rulers were indifferent to the colonies and would be glad to be rid of them.

The Whigs had been the main supporters of responsible government, and the Whigs were credited with the doctrine, which some at any rate of the leading men among them held, in common with

Radicals of the type of Richard Cobden, that complete separation of the colonies from the Mother Country was certainly inevitable and probably desirable. The Whigs were logical men, and separation was held to be the logical result of self-government and free trade. But family relations are neither logical nor illogical; they are human; and the family feeling which thinkers, writers, and politicians of the Whig School considered to be mere sentimentalism, was not mere sentimentalism, but common sense. The Whigs again, while professing democratic principles and fathering democratic measures, were essentially aristocratic, prim, and orthodox in their politics and their economic views. Hence the new type of somewhat raw democracy which came into being in the colonies, with its strong strain of Imperialism and its repudiation of *laissez-faire* doctrines, was not congenial to Whig statesmen. They were, therefore, minded to let the children drift apart, instead of being at pains to adjust the relations of youth and age. But human nature was too much for them, and family feeling asserted itself in friendly compromise between the young and the old.

Even at the present day, though the mischief of interference on the one hand, and of indifference on the other, is far better appreciated than it was forty or fifty years ago, the family relation, which is the human element in the Empire, might well be borne more constantly in mind. The criticism is often

made, if not in public utterance, at any rate in
private talk, that England has done much more for
the colonies than the colonies for England, that the
giving has all been on one side, and so forth. The
answer is that, if this is true, it is as it should be.
It is right and natural that the giving should be on
the parent's side. The *quid pro quo* comes in the
knowledge that the children will, if necessary, take
charge of the family in the coming time. As
a matter of fact, England has already received
substantial help from her children, as the record of
the South African war testifies ; and the Dominions
are now taking their part in the naval defence of
the Empire. But setting aside all considerations
of present gain, the fact remains that for the Mother
Country to give and the young peoples to receive is
in the course of nature.

There are many in England who are apt to be
impatient when domestic questions at issue in the
United Kingdom are criticized and canvassed overseas, not merely in the Press, but by leading politicians and even in the Legislatures. We read of
pronouncements being made or of resolutions being
passed on Home Rule, the House of Lords, Women's
Franchise, or some other burning question, and we
ask what would be said, if the House of Commons
were to pass a resolution on the relations of the
States or Provinces to the Federations, on the
Second Chamber Question, or on any other domestic
concern of one or other of the self-governing

Dominions. We are not ourselves wholly immune from a similar weakness; and from time to time we realize that domestic questions may easily wear the guise of Imperial questions, as when reciprocity with the United States was placed before the electors of Canada, and appealed to party feeling in England. But, assuming that the Dominions are more prone to pass public judgement on the Mother Country than the Mother Country on the Dominions, this also is in the course of nature. It is the privilege of the young to think that they can put the world to rights, and to criticize their elders; and if this holds true in private families, it holds equally true in a family of peoples.

If again we turn to the social relations between the English at home and the English over the seas, harmony in this all-important direction will be promoted and maintained only by bearing in mind the family analogy. Young men and women are sensitive, keenly alive to the difference of treatment which either makes them feel that they are tolerated and patronized or makes them feel at home. The same is true of members of young communities. The love of British men and women from over the seas for the Old Country will grow cold and turn to resentment if they hear themselves called, and feel themselves treated, as 'colonials', with the implication attached to the word that they are on a different level from their own folk at home. Every man and woman from the self-governing Dominions who visits England, goes back at the end of the visit an advocate for or against England. Either when they have come home—for coming to England is still termed coming home—they have found them-selves at home, or they have not; and they have found themselves at home in England only if they have been treated on family lines, with all the kindly feeling which is the natural outcome of youth and age making allowance for each other.

There are not a few who will still say with the Whigs of half a century ago that all this talk about the family is nothing more than talk, that these young peoples must go their ways, and the Mother Country go hers, as interest dictates; and there are perhaps more who see in the family analogy the bogy of Imperialism, whatever Imperialism means. The first is supposed to be the view of the plain business man. The second is the view of the man who hates national or racial bombast and exaggera-tion. The answer to the one is that dealings be-tween the young and the old peoples on family lines are good business; the answer to the other is that such dealings are the most natural thing in the world, opposed to anything that is spurious or affected. The good private business man looks to the future; and, looking to the future, he is glad to strengthen his business by family ties. The good public business man bears in mind the future possi-bilities of the young peoples, and realizes that separation of these young peoples from the Mother

Country cannot mean gain to her or to him and may mean grievous loss. There is a rational and an irrational Imperialism. Dislike of irrational and blatant Imperialism seems to breed a wrong-headed belief that to have a great and growing Empire, and to rejoice in it, is a sinful thing. It is no more sinful than to have a large and growing family; and pride in it is natural and healthy, when not combined with bluster and vulgar ostentation.

In short the one wise and sound way of looking at the Empire, so far as it consists of the Mother Country and the self-governing Dominions, of weighing its chances and estimating its future, is to argue from the family; and the one way to maintain and strengthen the family feeling and the family connexion is to bear in mind that the root of the matter is continuous adjustment between youth and age.

CHAPTER IV

SCIENCE AND EMPIRE

I. DISTANCE

In all previous eras distance has been the main obstacle to winning and keeping Empires. The great problem which leading nations and their leading men have during the centuries, one after another, set themselves to try to solve, has been how to hold together territories and peoples far removed from one another. Of all Empire builders and holders of the past the Romans were the most successful, and the Romans were pre-eminent in the attention which they paid to communications, in order, as far as possible, to counteract distance. ' The Romans were able for a long time to maintain the obedience of their provinces, and to suppress every attempt at resistance to their authority. This result was mainly due to the efficient military system of the Romans, and to the masterly manner in which they occupied a province, by stationing their legions in strong towns and fortified camps, and by making and maintaining their communications by means of the roads and bridges which they constructed.'[1] The roads were made, it should be noted, primarily

[1] Cornewall Lewis, *Government of Dependencies*, 1891 ed., p. 127.

for military purposes, not with the direct purpose of developing the resources of the countries through which they passed ; and soldiers on active service were often employed to make them, for, like the railway battalion in the Sudan, and the Italian troops in Erithrea, the Roman legionaries were soldiers of the line and Royal Engineers combined, and in the intervals between wars, their commander kept them in hand by employing them on Public Works.

But the world which the Romans conquered and held together was the Mediterranean world, and on the Mediterranean—it is important to remember— they had for their homeland the central peninsula. 'All the great Monarchies,' says Bacon, ' the Persians, the Romans (and the like of the Turks), they had not any provinces to the which they needed to demand access through the country of another ; neither had they any long races or narrow angles of territory, which were environed or clasped in with foreign states ; but their dominions were continued and entire, and had thickness and squareness in their orb or contents.' [1] 'The Provinces,' says Gibbon, ' surrounded and enclosed the Mediterranean ; and Italy, in the shape of an immense promontory, advanced into the midst of that great lake.' [2]

The Roman Empire, in fact, widened out from Rome as a centre, mainly on land. From the Forum

[1] Spedding's ed., vol. vii, p. 52; 'On the true greatness of the Kingdom of Britain.'
[2] *Decline and Fall*, chap. ii, 1862 ed., vol. i, p. 189.

at Rome the roads, strong and solid as their makers, radiated in straight lines to all parts of the Empire. When the sea intervened, it was a more or less adjoining sea, the shores of which had been known and settled for centuries. It is no doubt the case that, having on their hands—for instance—the whole of North Africa from Egypt to Mauretania, or again Britain, which was wholly outside the Mediterranean area, the Romans had in a sense to face the problem of holding and governing Provinces which were only accessible by crossing the sea; and Tacitus writes, with special reference to the East, of 'Provinciae, quae mari dividuntur'.[1]   It is also true, as will be noted below, that sea-going in Roman times was a far more dangerous and uncertain process than it is at the present day.   But, even when allowance has been made for the difference in scale and kind between the ancient and the modern world, Rome can hardly be said to have handled to any very appreciable extent distant overseas dependencies.   For the Romans distances were land distances rather than sea distances, and the Roman Empire could show no Province in relation to Rome even remotely comparable to Australia in its relation to England.   It was when Columbus had discovered America, and Europeans acquired great dependencies which were separated from the centre of Government by sea not by land, and by immense oceans not by the Mediterranean Sea or by the English Channel, that distance began

[1] *Annals*, ii. 43.

to play its most striking part as an obstacle to
Empire. There could then be no longer any question
of gradually widening out from a centre, of continuous advance, made good by prolonging existing
roads, of coasting along or crossing a long tried
inland sea. There was complete remoteness which,
as long as navigation was dependent on wind and
tide, that is for three centuries and more, was only
slightly modified by more skilful seamanship and
bigger and stronger ships. Distance accordingly
worked its full will on Empires. In some cases it
broke them up, and in all, so far as the Empires
were the products not of conquest merely but of
colonization also, it caused the white overseas
communities to develop distinct characteristics of
their own, inasmuch as, owing to distance, differences of surroundings, climate, and so forth were not
counteracted by close and constant contact with the
Motherland. It was not until after this element of
distance had had time to leave its mark upon the
Empires of the conquering and colonizing nations of
Europe, that the great enemy of distance appeared
on the scene in the form of scientific invention, and
steam and telegraphy began gradually to annihilate
space and time.

Now, the great question of the past having been
how to hold together peoples living at a great distance from each other, what is the answer to be
given to this question at the present day? The
answer is that all the signs of the times point to the

conclusion that in the days to come the question will cease to exist, that this element of distance will for practical purposes disappear altogether. No man, or, at any rate, no man unskilled in scientific learning, who studies what has been achieved in the past, can set any bounds to scientific achievement in the future. If, say, the cleverest man in Wolfe's army that fought on the Plains of Abraham in 1759 had been told that, had it all taken place a century and a half later, the news of the battle and of Wolfe's death, which occurred before noon on the 13th of September, instead of reaching London, as was actually the case, on the following 17th of October, would probably have been in the London evening papers on the actual day of the battle; and, if Canada had happened to be east instead of west of England, would have been in the English Press early on the same day; and further that he could himself probably have come back to London in a week, he would have treated his informant as a lunatic. How is it possible then, looking back on the past, to come to any other conclusion than that the process of annihilating distance will continue, and—so experience teaches us—at accelerated speed?

It is very noticeable how little space most writers and thinkers on political questions have given to the past results and the future possibilities of scientific invention as bearing upon politics. Lord Durham stands out almost alone as an exception to this rule. As his report shows, he contemplated, as far back as

1839, a time when 'the passage from Ireland to Quebec would be a matter of ten or twelve days ',[1] and he saw that the completion of satisfactory communication between Halifax and Quebec, especially if it was by rail, would make the union of the British North American provinces as they were in his day, not merely desirable but 'absolutely necessary'.[1] But in nearly every case the political expert, to all intents and purposes, reasons on the assumption that though human beings change, space and time and the main features of the world in which they live do not, which may be literally true, but is practically incorrect.

It was more or less true before modern science made itself felt. Consequently, the Romans in dealing with their Provinces dealt, so to speak, with a fixed unit. On the other hand, those who are handling the British Empire are dealing with a fluctuating and uncertain unit. If, for instance, we take a Roman colony removed from Rome by both land and sea, the distance of Rome from Eboracum, the modern York, remained much the same, in the sense of the time required for covering the distance, for the whole time that Britain was a Roman Province, in other words, for at least three and a half centuries. Once the roads were made in Italy, Gaul, and Britain, any difference in the distance between the two points at one time as compared with another depended solely upon the comparative

---

[1] 1912 ed., vol. ii, pp. 318–19.

military efficiency of the Romans at one time and another, with the resulting state of the roads and the safety or insecurity of the travelling. On the other hand, take Toronto, once called York, in Canada. Though it had been the site of a French fort at an earlier date, as a city it was born about the year 1793, when General Simcoe was Lieutenant-Governor of Upper Canada. Its distance from London at the present day, 120 years since it was founded, if measured by the travelling of human beings, is certainly not more than a sixth of what it was in Simcoe's time, and as measured by telegraphic communication has become almost non-existent. Thus the relations between London and Toronto have been constantly changing, always, it is true, in the same direction, that of greater proximity, but none the less changing, and, therefore, the problem of Empire has been constantly changing likewise.

On the other hand, while the gradual diminution of distance makes a modern Empire, as compared with an Empire of the past, a more fluctuating and less constant unit, the improved and improving communication, which produces as its direct result this element of change, is in itself a more constant and certain factor than the communication which existed in past times. The importance of steam communication, especially on the sea, consists not only in ensuring greater speed, but also in ensuring greater regularity. A mail steamer crossing the Atlantic meets with heavy weather.   She arrives at her port of destination possibly a good many hours behind time.   But the delay and uncertainty is as nothing compared with communication by sailing-ships.   The historian of ' the Romans under the Empire' tells us that, before the days of steam, 'in fair seasons, and with fair winds, the navigation of the ancients, conducted by oars and sails, was speedier than our own,' but that, on the other hand, storm or adverse winds prolonged the voyages almost indefinitely; while in winter time the sea was closed.   'The communication between Italy and Spain by water was interrupted in the middle of November and only recommenced in March.'[1]   Now that steamers have taken the place of sailing-ships, certainty has been substituted for uncertainty; steam is the master, not the wind or the sea.   Thus it may be summed up that the Romans were called upon to counteract permanently fixed distances by more or less uncertain methods. The English are dealing with continually changing distances by more or less assured and constant, though always quickening, machinery.

Telegraphy deserves special notice in connexion with the subject of communications and Empire. The speed of the post was in Roman times, and is in our own, the speed of the fastest travelling human being.   A man travels faster now than he did in Roman times, because he travels on land or sea by

[1] Merivale, *History of the Romans under the Empire*, 1865 ed., chap. xxxix, vol. iv, pp. 390–1.

steam, instead of on or behind horses and in sailing-
ships.   A post is carried faster for the same reason.
But whether the letters are carried by relays of
mounted couriers, as among the Persians and the
Romans, or by railways, the letter travels no faster
than man, assuming the man to have sufficient
endurance.   Letters are sent from London, via
Brindisi, to catch the mail steamers for India and
Australia at Port Said, but a man can travel by the
same route and arrive in the same time.   Thus, if
we take steam alone, although steam communication
is from one point of view wholly different in kind
from communication by horses on land and sailing-
ships on sea, from another point of view it differs
not so much in kind as in degree, for the speed of
posts in relation to men has remained constant,
being as a matter of fact one and the same for letters
and for human beings.   But when we come to
telegraphy, we have reached a species of communication which is ever so much more remote than
steam from old-world communication, for it bears
no relation whatever to the travelling speed of
a human being.   In other words, modern science
has not merely accelerated and regularized communication, measured, so to speak, by the standard
of human beings, but has evolved a new species of
communication in which the standard of the human
being has disappeared altogether.

What further developments may be in store in
this direction ; what the conquest of the air, which

is now beginning, may bring to birth; and whether the human standard of communication may in generations to come be levelled up towards the non-human or telegraphic standard, must be left either to pure speculation or to the forecast of the greatest scientific men. We can be content for the present purpose with the plain and patent fact that distance is constantly growing less, and with the inevitable conclusion that the great Empire problem of the past, which was a problem of distance, will cease to exist.

What will be the result? The result, it seems, will be that, while the old standing difficulty of Empire will be removed, the agency which has removed or is removing it, will create, and already is creating, new difficulties, to tax the brains of statesmen and the patience of citizens. Let us take elimination of distance as affecting, firstly, the relations between the Self-Governing Dominions and the Mother Country, secondly, the internal relations of the Empire as a whole, and, thirdly, the relations between the Empire and the outside world.

It has already been pointed out that elimination of distance is coming too late in the day to neutralize the effect which distance has produced in making more or less separate nations. The Self-Governing Dominions have taken their present form and shape because of distance. They were set to govern themselves because the Mother Country, being distant, could not otherwise satisfactorily provide for their government. Before the modern doctrine of responsible government was propounded and put into practice, it was suggested that the British over-seas communities might send representatives to the British Parliament. This suggestion was ridiculed by Edmund Burke as being impracticable on the ground of distance. It would not be impracticable now to anything like the same extent, and in one or two generations will probably not be impracticable at all. But, on the other hand, if representatives were sent to an Imperial Parliament at the present day, they would come as representing distinct nations which distance has brought into existence. In other words, their presence in England would not now be, as it would have been in Burke's time, in lieu of self-government in the Dominions, but additional to and supplementing self-government. Moreover, again as the result of distance working for another century and a half since Burke wrote, the representatives, assuming them to be of the same British race, would yet be more or less distinct types of the race. No doubt the diminution of dis-tance is modifying and will in a growing degree modify the divergence, but still we have to reckon with the broad fact that even when distance has been eliminated, the results of distance will endure.

It has been suggested in a previous chapter that the diversity in the British Provinces of the British Empire which great spaces have promoted, may eventually be found to be rather a source of strength than of weakness, making for union, not for discord. Conversely, the elimination of distance may not be and probably will not be wholly a gain. Relations can see too much of each other, and familiarity is said to breed contempt. More intimate and every-day knowledge of one another means, or may mean, greater emphasis on the differences which have been produced by different surroundings. Every change in human relations, however, has its bad as well as its good side, and it cannot seriously be doubted that the net result of the elimination of distance must be to promote harmony between Great Britain and the Self-Governing Dominions. Increased coming and going must mean better understanding; the vacant spaces will be filled by British citizens less and less moulded by distance, and, therefore, not increasing but diminishing the divergence; while the dangers of proximity which arise from facilities for interference, are now practically non-existent as far as regards the Self-Governing Dominions, owing to the fact that distance has done its work in creating distinct peoples and demonstrating the futility and unwisdom of one people interfering in the domestic concerns of another.

If, however, we turn to consider the internal relations of the Empire as a whole, it is not possible to feel equal confidence as to the results of elimination of distance. The fact must be faced that while it probably makes for better relations between the white citizens of the Empire, it tends to widen the gulf between the white British citizens of the Self-Governing Dominions, and the coloured British citizens of India and the Crown Colonies. The closer India comes to British North America, Australasia, and South Africa, the more prominent and aggressive becomes the colour problem. We should hear little of it, were these lands now as remote from each other as they were 100 years ago, and even now we should hear less of it, were Canada and Australia as thickly populated with white men and women as is the United Kingdom. But, as things are, the growing proximity of white men's lands with empty spaces to lands over-populated with coloured men, tends gravely to emphasize the fact, to which further reference will be made in a later chapter, that the British Empire is two Empires in one, and to make the instinct of race run counter to the bond of citizenship. The Romans have given us no guidance in this matter, for they do not seem to have been troubled to an appreciable extent by any colour difficulty, and, at any rate, if they had a problem of the kind, they did not find it accentuated by lessening of distance.

This difficulty is mainly a difficulty as between the different overseas Provinces, and does not immediately concern the Mother Country, except so far as it is vital to the whole Empire. Let us therefore go on to note what effect the growing elimination of distance has on the relations between the United Kingdom and the Tropical possessions of

the Crown.   Beyond question constant and speedy
communication in the main facilitates administration and strengthens control, but at the same time
it also facilitates interference, by the Home Government with the men on the spot ; by Parliament,
the general public, and the Press, with the Government; and so far it tends to weaken the executive,
to militate against continuity which is vital for the
keeping of an Empire.   It gives rise to more knowledge of one kind and to less of another.   There is
far more going to and fro in the present than there
was in the past, and a much larger proportion of
Englishmen know something of India than was
the case a century ago.   But, on the other hand, the
Englishmen set to rule or to trade in India make
India less of a home than in bygone days, when
visits to England were necessarily few and at long
intervals of years.   The tendency to come back
constantly during the course of service is stronger
than it was, because the opportunities of returning
are greater ; and the English in India, therefore, are
less of India than they were, in the sense of passing
their working lives unbrokenly amid Indian surroundings.   Nor, again, are the multiplied visits to
England of the King's coloured Indian subjects, and
the consequently growing familiarity of East Indians
with the Englishman at home, all a gain to them
or to us.   In any case, if we allow that quicker
and more constant communication between East
and West, or between Africa and England, is not

only inevitable but on the whole beneficial, we must at the same time allow that it is making the problem of Empire infinitely more complicated.

As distance diminishes within the Empire, so it diminishes at the same rate between any or all parts of the Empire and the outside world. What is the result? The Self-Governing Dominions are being brought closer to England and to each other, but *pari passu* they are being brought closer to foreign nations. It would at first sight seem that constant contact between two different races or nationalities might tend to weaken the instinct of race; but that instinct is so strong that closer contact and therefore sharper contrast may possibly rather intensify it. It may be said, perhaps, with more confidence that the elimination of distance will tend on the whole to strengthen the race instinct, than that this tendency will necessarily make for unity in the Empire. Strong race feeling may make white citizens within the Empire range themselves with white men outside the Empire as against coloured fellow-citizens within the Empire, and conversely the latter may turn towards coloured peoples who do not share their citizenship in preference to white British peoples who ignore it as a bond of sympathy or brotherhood. Take again the white races only, so far as the white men in the Self-Governing Dominions are not British, improved communication which brings the French Canadians closer not only to England but to their old mother - land France,

may make them not less but more French, and
so with the Dutchmen in South Africa. Or take
once more the British race alone. Australia is
being brought closer to the United States as well
as to England, a young British nation, to another
kindred nation young as compared with England
and correspondingly attractive in various ways.

Assume, however, that elimination of distance
will not be a dissolving factor as regards the British
Empire, soldiers and sailors must still be asked
what effect it will have in case of war. To a lay-
man it would seem that, inasmuch as the British
Empire is and has been specially vulnerable in
virtue of being so widely spread, the concentration
which will be the result of eliminating distance will
make it easier to defend in case of attack, notwithstanding that the possible enemies on all sides are
being brought closer to our doors.

One notable result of the lessening of distance
for the British Empire in particular, and for the
world in general, is what may be called the rise
of the South. It is through the lessening and
elimination of distance, and only through it, that
the lands in the Southern Seas, so remote from the
main centres of the world, are at length beginning
to take their part in making history. The East
led the way; civilization moved West and North;
then further West across the Atlantic to the New
World; and now far in the Southern hemisphere,
the Argentine Republic, South Africa, and above

all Australasia, are beginning to loom large on the horizon. Of the three groups of British Self-Governing Dominions two are in the South, and the rise of the South, as distance decreases, peculiarly concerns Great Britain and her Empire.

In this chapter, as in the whole little book, no pretence is made to elaborate solutions of the great problems of the future. It is only desired to suggest what those problems may be and how they have arisen or are arising. As regards the special subject of this chapter, distance and Empire, it seems safe to sum up ; that science is determining and will determine the fate and the kind of Empires : that science is removing what has been the greatest of all impediments to Empires in the past, and in turn is creating new difficulties : and that the Empires of the past, in the absence of modern science, presented a more difficult problem in the sense that the one great obstacle to a solution was more overwhelming, but an easier problem in the sense that the conditions were far less complex.

CHAPTER V

SCIENCE AND EMPIRE

(ii) WATER AND MEDICAL SCIENCE

IN the last chapter no reference was made to canals as agents in counteracting distance, because canals, being merely water roads instead of land roads, do not necessarily imply steam and electricity. Yet, to take the most obvious instances, the Suez Canal is, and the Panama Canal, when completed, will be, of the utmost importance in bringing different parts of the world closer together. Reference has been made above to the fact that the component parts of the British Empire are, by the agency of science, being brought closer to foreign nations as well as to one another. One most important result of the Panama Canal will be to bring Australia and New Zealand nearer by sea to the great ports on the Eastern coast of the United States than to Great Britain.

Canals of one kind or another, in the sense of large ditches or waterways dug out between one water and another, are presumably as old as human activity in any form. In China and Egypt, for instance, there were canals from very early dates, for transport as well as for irrigation. The canal from the Nile to the Red Sea, connecting the Red Sea and the Mediterranean, which was finally opened by Ptolemy Philadelphus about two and a half centuries B.C., had been begun about 600 years B.C. and possibly much earlier. The story told us by Herodotus of Xerxes' canal through the peninsula of Mount Athos—'velificatus Athos'—is a good instance of an ancient ship canal; and a canal through the Isthmus of Corinth is said to have been contemplated by Periander about 600 B.C. as well as later by Caesar and by Nero.

But the Romans, who set an example to all time of road- and bridge-making and of bringing drinking water on aqueducts, do not appear to have made conspicuous use of canals for what may be called Imperial purposes. Mommsen tells us that Ptolemy's canal was kept open and navigable in Roman times, but that it 'was in the Roman period only of secondary rank, employed chiefly perhaps for the conveyance of blocks of marble and porphyry from the Egyptian east coast to the Mediterranean'.[1] From Tacitus we learn that one of the Roman generals in Nero's time, in order to give his soldiers something to do in time of peace, designed a canal to connect the Moselle and the Saone, 'so that troops crossing the sea and then conveyed on the Rhone and Arar (Saone) might sail by this canal into the Moselle and the Rhine, and thence to the

---

[1] *The Provinces of the Roman Empire*, English translation, vol. ii, p. 297.

ocean. Thus the difficulties of the route being removed, there would be communication for ships between the shores of the West and of the North.'[1] But this canal was never made; and the first great artificial water communications carried out in France date from the seventeenth century, the Briare canal, connecting the Loire and the Seine, and the Languedoc canal, or *Canal du Midi*, 140 miles long, linking the Gulf of Lyons to the Bay of Biscay.

The Romans seem to have repaired and improved existing canals, especially in Egypt, but the canals which were entirely their own work were mainly local canals. There was, for instance, the Fossa Mariana at the mouth of the Rhone, the handiwork of the Republican general, Marius. Augustus made a canal in connexion with his great naval station at Ravenna. Tacitus tells us of another Roman general who kept his soldiers employed in digging 'a canal of 23 miles in length between the Rhine and the Meuse, as a means of avoiding the uncertain perils of the ocean'.[2] This, according to the commentator, was a canal near the coast of Holland, possibly in the neighbourhood of Leyden, and its object was not so much to facilitate transport as to prevent inundation of the land by the sea. There were again in our own fen districts and Lincolnshire the Caer Dyke and the Foss Dyke, 40 miles long

[1] Tacitus, *Annals*, xiii. 53, Church and Brodribb's translation.

[2] *Annals*, xi. 20, Church and Brodribb's translation. See the note to the passage.

and $10\frac{1}{2}$ miles long respectively; but these too were local waterways, and it may safely be said that canals for purposes of long distance traffic did not figure to any appreciable extent in the organization of the Roman Empire. The reason was twofold. In the first place, communications with the Romans were primarily a military matter, and canals would have been of little use to them for the purpose of moving their legions promptly from one place to another. In the second place, neither the Romans, nor any of the ancient peoples, seem to have had any idea of using locks to adjust differences of level in water communication. Locks hardly imply a very advanced stage of engineering knowledge, and it seems extraordinary that they only came into use in modern times. To what extent they have been utilized in the British Empire with the aid of modern machinery can be realized by those who have seen the traffic at the Sault Ste Marie between Lake Superior and Lake Huron, or at home have noted the Manchester ship canal, described in 1896 as 'the first large ship canal which has been constructed with locks, raising the vessels $60\frac{1}{2}$ feet, and transporting them inland, and thereby converting an inland city into a seaport'.[1]

Inland water communication in the British Empire has found its fullest expression in Canada. The Roman Empire contained no Province which could be set side by side with Canada in this respect.

[1] Harcourt's *Rivers and Canals*, 1896, vol. ii, p. 592.

In Canada, before the days of railways, roughly speaking down to the middle of the nineteenth century, communication was by water rather than by land, and inland canals have played, and still play, a notably great part in the history of the Dominion.   They have been used at once to supplement and correct the natural waterways, and to shorten distance.   There are 73 miles of canal correcting the great waterway between Lake Superior and the Gulf of St. Lawrence, and some 48 locks, Lake Superior being 600 feet above the level of the sea.   The canal which would have the greatest effect in shortening distance was talked of in Lord Durham's time and before, but is still for the future. This is the Georgian Bay canal, which would link Lake Huron to the St. Lawrence at Montreal, by following the Ottawa river and the old French route to the West.   Canadian canals are mostly of no great length.   They began with short cuts on the St. Lawrence, above Montreal, constructed, it should be noted, in the Roman spirit, for military purposes, when a military man, General Haldimand, was Governor ; and in the Rideau canal, which was carried out at a later date, 126 miles long, from Ottawa to Kingston, we have again a work on Roman lines, in that it was made for purely military reasons, an Imperial undertaking paid for by the Imperial Government.   Possibly, if the Romans had found their way to Canada, Eastern Canada being so fashioned that its natural highways are water highways, they might have turned their attention to communication by water rather than by land, and might have invented locks. But they would have had to leaven their military instincts with a larger amount of commercial initiative than appears in their history, to have constructed, for instance, the 27 miles of Welland canal for the purpose of carrying not troops and their provisions but heavy merchandise past the falls of Niagara. That canal, too, though not in its present form, was, like the Rideau canal, anterior to railways. Its present form, and the great canals of modern days, we owe to steam in the making, and they carry steamers when made.

Now, leaving altogether the subject of communication, let us ask what science contributed in other directions to the Roman Empire, and how far it has transformed and is likely still farther to transform our own Empire. It may be laid down in general terms that, over and above communication, the main Empire work of science is to make habitable places more habitable and unhabitable places habitable. But, before taking this point, it is necessary to say a word as to the influence of science in causing the transplantation of human beings, not only directly by easier communications, but also indirectly, as the result of scientific inventions.

Ages before the Romans came to mould the world, stupendous works, some of public utility, some apparently little better than private freaks, were made by human hands, and are standing, like the Pyramids, to astonish us still, but it would be hard to say how far they were the result of scientific invention and how far the outcome of unlimited application of brute force, at a time when despotism and slavery were in their most naked stage. Science or force must have temporarily peopled particular localities, only to be left derelict again ; but it is impossible to reason from these very far back days as from the records of the comparatively modern Roman Empire.

It can be taken that in historical times, in the ordinary course, the ancients, like the moderns, found at this or that place one metal or another of commercial value and had learnt how to smelt and to work it. The finding attracted population to the spot ; means were devised for providing the new-comers adequately with food and water ; and when the mines were exhausted, so far as science then reached, the population moved away. That process has presumably been common to all ages, as well as the process of this or that town acquiring or losing, from one local cause or another, a particular industry. But modern invention and modern appliances in machinery must have vastly increased the scale on which, and the rate at which, the populating and depopulating have taken place. Moreover, the fact that mines in the Roman Empire were treated wholly or mainly as State property and were leased by the Government, may have had to some extent the effect of preventing great rushes of adventurers eager to peg out claims. At any rate, we do not read of any Kimberley or Johannesburg or Kalgoorlie or Dawson City springing up in the Roman Empire. Ruins of what seem to have been considerable mining centres exist in Eastern Egypt near the coast of the Red Sea. But the remains prove that here the Romans were in no sense pioneers : they only continued existing workings. Moreover, these mining townships or cantonments were situated on or near a caravan route from the Red Sea to the Nile, in a fine strategic position commanding the water supply of the district, which points to the conclusion that population may have been attracted on other grounds than mining alone.

Nor again do we find any analogy in the Roman Empire to the effect upon the working population which the substitution of machinery for hand labour has produced in modern times. For instance, in the twenties and thirties of the last century there was a large stream of emigration to British North America from the North of England and the South of Scotland. One great cause of the movement was the distress which arose among the weavers of Lancashire, Lanark, and Renfrew in consequence of the substitution of machinery for hand labour. This was a case in which scientific invention repelled population and led to its being transplanted to America.

We read that *latifundia perdidere Italiam*, that the economic effect of large estates worked by slave

labour was to depopulate some districts of agricultural Italy, to drive out the small freeholder or
peasant farmer. We read too of the cities of the
Roman Empire, or, at any rate, of Rome itself, with
its superior attractions, depleting the country, just
as London and the great urban centres do at the
present day ; but there does not seem to be evidence
that the movement of population in the Roman
Empire was, to any appreciable extent, affected by
scientific invention.

A German authority has been quoted to the effect
that 'most of the realms of the ancient Roman
Empire had better connexions and conditions than
ever afterwards or even now '.[1]   If this is true, how
far was it the result of scientific knowledge among
the Romans, and how far did they apply science to
making the habitable parts of their Empire more
habitable, and unhabitable places habitable? Allowance must be made not only for the results of
human injury or neglect, but also for changes which
since their day nature has wrought or may have
wrought in lands or localities which they tamed
and civilized. The sea, for instance, has left Ravenna
inland and derelict. Gibbon writes of it, 'The
gradual retreat of the sea has left the modern city
at the distance of four miles from the Adriatic, and
as early as the fifth or sixth century of the Christian

[1] Heinrich Stephan as quoted in Friedländer's *Roman Life and
Manners under the Early Empire* (authorized translation), vol. i,
p. 268.

era the port of Augustus was converted into pleasant
orchards, and a lonely grove of pines covered the
ground where the Roman fleet once rode at anchor.'[1]
Climate again may have changed in one district or
another, apart from the undoing of man. It must
also be borne in mind that, though the Roman
Empire eventually included no doubt much that
might be classed comparatively as bush or back-
wood, the proportion was as nothing compared with
the wild lands overseas which the English have
taken in hand. Yet the Romans had wide scope
for applying such scientific knowledge as they
possessed, and they possessed a great deal. Their
noble bridges and aqueducts, as well as their roads,
testify that they were good engineers. They knew
how to drain lands for agriculture and for sanitation.
They made embankments and dykes and reclaimed
from the sea. In various parts of what was their
Empire the ground which they made was subse-
quently lost and even now has not been recovered.
But the same is true of countries which they never
administered. In Ceylon, for instance, the English
are painfully restoring the great tanks and water-
courses which once irrigated and made fruitful
districts that afterwards relapsed into jungle. All
the world over, much of the good work of the past
has been lost; but taking the Roman Empire as the
most highly organized system of the ancient world
in historical times, there does not seem to have been

[1] Chap. xxx, 1862 ed., vol. iv, p. 42.

what has marked modern history and colonization, at any rate since steam and electricity have been brought into play, a constant onward movement of science, a continual perfecting of old inventions, and series of new discoveries. What the Romans knew, they knew well; and what they did, they did well; but after all their knowledge was comparatively limited and their aims were comparatively limited also.

Roman aims were limited for two reasons already given. The first reason was that, taking their history as a whole and their Empire as a whole, with the Romans military considerations were paramount. This does not mean that their Empire was purely the outcome of deliberate conquest and annexation on a preconceived plan. They were drawn on in the path of Empire, as we have been drawn on, by force of circumstances. Nor again does it mean that all the Provinces were simply held down by military garrisons. On the contrary, in the Provinces not on the frontiers of the Empire, after the time of Augustus, as a rule no legions were quartered; and the letters of Cicero at one time, of Pliny at another, show that economic and social questions received as much attention as, or more than, military matters. Merchants, traders, financiers, and speculators of all kinds, were coming and going and operating throughout the Roman Empire as through ours; and the Government had its eye on commerce, on national and provincial sources and methods of production. But it seems true to say that, while the Romans largely developed, partially colonized, wonderfully assimilated, and in some cases, or at some periods, effectively administered the countries which they had conquered, their ultimate object was to secure and maintain their tenure. Their military strength and their comparative toleration made for peace and consequently for development, and so did their military roads and their strongly guarded towns ; while men of the type of Agricola in Britain—a soldier in a frontier Province—had in full measure the desire and the capacity to be good and workmanlike governors, to study the interests of the ruled as well as the rulers. But, none the less, it may fairly be said that development was more of a by-product with the Romans than it is with us. 'It was no part of the policy of the conquerors', writes Merivale, 'to facilitate the intercourse of the natives of the interior.'[1] It is true that our primary object in India is to hold India ; but development of India, not merely for its advantages to England, but at least as much for the benefit of India and the Indians, is the aim of those who have charge of it. India is less exclusively regarded from a military point of view than would have been the case, had it been a Roman Province. It is less a piece on a military chess-board than it would have been in Roman hands.

[1] *History of the Romans under the Empire*, vol. iv, chap. xxxix, p. 400.

The second reason was that the Romans did not deal or attempt to deal with great areas of territory to the same extent and in the same sense as modern nations, the English in particular. This was partly because the areas were as a matter of fact infinitely smaller, one British Province alone (Canada) being apparently about double the size of the whole Roman Empire,[1] partly because in the areas which the Romans ruled, their *métier* was, as has been seen, not to spread, but to concentrate, again largely because they were first and foremost soldiers. The Roman Wall in Northumberland seems to illustrate the Imperial policy of Rome. The remains of it stand after all the centuries to tell us how strongly the Romans built, how well they did the work to which they put their hands. But why was it built? To give security, to enable them to hold what they had, and to hold it as a military people. Walls are made to keep some human beings in and other human beings out. They do not facilitate but obstruct coming and going. They are not means of development, they are obstacles to development except so far as they give security to the enclosed area. The Roman Wall meant a preserve for barbarism outside it. We may find some rough analogy, perhaps, on the northern frontier of India, where various

[1] Gibbon at the end of his first chapter says that the Roman Empire in the time of the Antonines ' was supposed to contain above sixteen hundred thousand square miles ', but his note to the passage shows that he distrusted the figures. Canada is given an area of nearly 3¾ million square miles.

native States are secluded from the indiscriminate coming and going of white men ; and in lands where British supremacy has been assured, in South or East Africa, for instance, or in New Zealand, native reserves have been established to safeguard the interests of the indigenous races. But, taken as a whole, British trade and colonization have known no limits. The policy has not been that of the Roman Wall.

The Roman aqueducts can be taken as evidence of Roman scientific knowledge and engineering skill. If the Romans did not make much use of canals for long distance traffic, they were past masters in bringing water for drinking purposes. How far in this matter did they, as the saying is, think and work Imperially? How far did they make habitable places more habitable, or unhabitable places habitable? The answer seems to be that they achieved the first object more than the second, that they handled mainly, though not exclusively, places already populated, and colonized largely in existing towns. By their aqueducts they more often improved than created. We should find it difficult to match in strength and beauty the magnificent aqueducts which supplied Rome itself with water, or the Pont du Gard which supplied Nismes, and whose 'lightness of structure, combined with such prodigious durability, produces the strongest sense of science and self-reliant power in the men who designed it'. 'None but Romans', added John

Addington Symonds, ' could have built such a monu-
ment and have set it in such a place.'[1]   But it was
built to supply a town in one of the most civilized
parts of the Roman Empire, hard by Provence
which specially appropriated to itself the generic
term of 'Provincia'.   The records of the Roman
Empire would not provide a parallel to the water-
supply of Kalgoorlie in Western Australia.   That
is an instance of making a place far remote in an
outlying Province of the Empire, not on a trade-
route, not on the fringe of but in the heart of the
desert, not merely habitable but the scene of a considerable modern city with the latest conveniences
and appliances, by bringing water from the Mundar-
ing reservoir, which even Rome might have envied,
in pipes for 350 miles.

Again, so far as their aqueducts and water-courses
served agricultural purposes, irrigating fields and not
merely supplying fountains and baths in cities, the
Romans seem rather to have improved and supplemented existing conditions than to have evolved
something wholly new.   They are not associated to
the same extent as Eastern peoples with large irrigation schemes, though a quotation to the contrary is
given below.[2]   Augustus, who kept the Province of
Egypt in his own hands, took care that the canal
system of the country was repaired and completed,
and Mommsen writes that 'the Roman Government

---

[1] *Sketches and Studies in Italy and Greece*, First Series, 1898 ed.,
chapter on 'Old Towns of Provence ', p. 76.   [2] p. 65.

applied itself more zealously to the elevation of agriculture in Egypt than anywhere else';[1] but notwithstanding, Roman engineers do not seem to have left any very distinctive mark upon the land of the Nile and now of the Assouan dam. Nor did they anywhere, in the matter of irrigation, rival the triumphs of British engineers and the British Government in India. There Sir Bampfylde Fuller tells us that 'from irrigation works maintained by the State seventeen million acres are irrigated—an area half the size of England'. 'Not only do these canals increase prosperity; they create it. Two of the Punjâb canals literally have converted desolate uninhabited plains into thriving countries. Along the Chenâb canal now stretch fields and villages inhabited by a million people, where twelve years ago a few nomads wandered over a desert of parched earth and camel thorn. The State irrigation works of India are, of their kind, the greatest and most beneficent triumphs of engineering that the world has seen.'[2]

There were no doubt cases in which, by draining, reclamation, and irrigation, the Romans did creative work, making land existent, which for men to dwell in and for productive purposes had been non-existent before they came. To Roman handiwork, for instance, aided by the receding sea, we owe the

[1] *The Provinces of the Roman Empire*, vol. ii, p. 253.
[2] *Studies of Indian Life and Sentiment*, by Sir Bampfylde Fuller, K.C.S.I., C.I.E., 1910, pp. 322 and 195.

rich cornland of Romney Marsh. 'Parts of Algeria, now wholly barren, were fertile and populous, owing to their unsurpassed system of irrigation,' and 'modern travellers notice with astonishment the ruins of what must have been flourishing cities far beyond the present limits of Algerian civilization'.[1] In the Hauran, east of the Jordan, they built, irrigated, and reclaimed. 'At this eastern limit of the Empire there was gained for Hellenic civilization a frontier domain which may be compared with the Romanized region of the Rhine.'[2]   But in the Hauran, as in Eastern Egypt, they were not the first pioneers, and their beneficent work seems to have been done on or near caravan or trade-routes.

Perhaps it may be summed up that the Romans set themselves to make the best use of water which was on the spot, and to bring to the spot water which was within comparatively easy reach.   But, even where it was a question of existing water, in the absence of modern appliances, no large river was controlled by them, to anything like the same extent that the Nile has been by the great works of latter days; and where it was a question of bringing water to where water was not, the supply was brought to a limited area and from a short distance away.   The Romans had the Libyan desert on their frontier, but they had no call to try and reclaim more than its fringes.   They were not faced with,

[1] Arnold's *Roman Provincial Administration*, pp. 44, 229.
[2] Mommsen, *The Provinces of the Roman Empire*, vol. ii, p. 158.

and did not attempt to handle on a large scale, the problem how to make a desert not a desert, which is the problem that faces us in the interior of Australia, and which, if ever solved, will make the rise of the South more important than ever in the history of the world. Here we have a Province, which is in itself a continent, greater in size than the Roman Empire, and the future of this continent is mainly a question of water supply. Water means population, and production, and, therefore, science will in a unique degree determine the position of Australia among the nations of the world. An instance has been given, in Western Australia, of bringing water from a long distance, measured by the surface of the earth. Elsewhere, especially in Queensland, we have water brought from a comparatively long distance within the earth, by artesian wells, which would not have been possible without the aid of modern machinery. The great central artesian basin in Australia is estimated to extend over more than half a million of square miles and to underlie more than half the State of Queensland. The boring has been carried down to a depth of 5,000 feet, not very far short of a mile. Thus underground water is being made available to an extent wholly unknown to the ancients. How far the supply will be permanent, or how far a not unlimited stock is being depleted, has yet to be fully proved; but the measurements which have so far been made of the flows of the artesian bores point distinctly to

a decrease in the supply. This is a case of mining
for water, which would be useless, if the water were
not there already. It is for the future to determine
whether by human ingenuity a purely waterless
region can be made water-bearing; and also whether
the art of turning salt water into fresh by the
process of condensing, which again was apparently
unknown to the Romans, can be applied upon any
large scale.

Water is one great agency in making unhabitable
places habitable, and habitable places more habitable.
Another is medical science. When the history of
the British Empire for the past thirty years comes
to be written; if it is written aright, one of the
leading features in the story will be the rise of
medical science into the front rank of human
agencies which are making and keeping Empires.
The lifetime of a middle-aged man at the present
day covers the main part of the discoveries connected
with the germ theory of disease, the work of
Pasteur, Lister, Koch, Laveran, and others, carried
forward more especially in the British Empire by
Manson, Ross, Bruce, Boyce, and their fellow
workers. Lord Lister, who has but lately died,
in the latter part of his life, when he had revolution-
ized surgery, gave his great name and influence
to the movement for combating tropical diseases;
and science received support from statesmanship—
the strong support of Mr. Chamberlain, as Secretary
of State for the Colonies. The movement is still in

its infancy, but the discovery that flies and mosquitoes are the conductors of disease, that the anopheline mosquito—as indicated by Sir Patrick Manson and proved by Sir Ronald Ross—is the bearer of malaria, that the stegomyia is the medium of yellow fever, that the tsetse fly infects horses and cattle, that one or more species of that fly are the agents for spreading sleeping sickness among human beings; all these and kindred discoveries hold out promise that the future record of the tropical dependencies of European nations will be widely different from the past.

We find no analogy to what is now taking place in the history of the Roman Empire. The Romans had plenty of common sense and rare power of organization. They were well alive to the calls of public health, to the virtues of fresh air, of pure drinking water, and of good sewers. They knew that marshes cause fever: they even connected disease with insects bred in marshes, and mosquito nets are mentioned by Roman classical writers.[1] They or those whom they ruled, the Greeks and others, had considerable knowledge of medicine and surgery. There were writers on medical subjects, consulting physicians with large practices, and medical officers of health.[2] But there seems to

---

[1] See *The Prevention of Malaria*, by Sir Ronald Ross, 1910, chap. i, pp. 5–6.

[2] 'The regular organization of public medical attendance in the Provinces dates from Antoninus Pius, who required the towns of Asia to have a certain number of physicians among their salaried officers.' Dill's *Roman Society from Nero to Marcus Aurelius*, 2nd ed., 1905, p. 219.

be no record of their making any great discovery of the cause and the prevention of some widespread disease in man or animal, which would have effect on whole Provinces or groups of Provinces. They evidently came across malaria in Campania, where Pompey caught fever, but what Gibbon terms 'the fertile and happy Province of Campania, the scene of the early victories and of the delicious retirements of the citizens of Rome',[1] must have been—possibly because it was better drained—widely different from the Roman Campagna of our own day, the home of malaria and, be it noted, the scene where in 1900 it was proved to demonstration that remaining at night time in a mosquito-proof dwelling confers immunity from malarial fever.

The Romans, it must be again repeated, conquered and held in subjection large areas, but for practical purposes handled only towns and small areas. They were very rarely pioneers. They did not settle far afield, or stray into jungle or bush. Nor did they administer tropical dependencies, lands where European new-comers were in danger of their lives from climatic causes. In other words, medical science among the Romans was not called upon to serve Imperial purposes to any appreciable extent, or, perhaps, it would be more correct to say that the Imperial purposes which medicine served among

[1] Chap. xvii, 1862 ed., vol. ii, p. 336. See on the subject of Campania in Roman times, Pelham's *Essays on Roman History*, chap. xii, 'Discoveries at Rome', pp. 268-74.

the Romans were smaller and narrower than ours. The most that medicine did for the Roman Empire was to keep the soldiers as far as possible in good health, and to keep the towns and small highly planted and civilized areas in good sanitary order.

If we take our own Empire, we find that medical science is working its beneficial results on a large scale in all the tropical and subtropical dependencies, as well as in Egypt. Malta fever, for instance, which has a far wider area than Malta or even the Mediterranean, since Sir David Bruce's Commission traced its origin to parasites, conveyed in goats' milk, has, where the use of that milk has been discontinued, almost entirely disappeared. India and the Far East, the West Indies, the North of Australia—all the tropics are becoming healthier for white men and coloured alike ; but perhaps the healing art, now become the preventive science, is doing its greatest work in tropical Africa, the land of the tsetse fly, of blackwater fever, of malaria, of sleeping sickness, of yellow fever, and many other diseases. What is medical science doing for this continent? It is making the parts which were unhabitable for Europeans, or barely habitable, comparatively safe for them to live in. It cannot make a tropical climate not tropical, but it can transform, and is already largely transforming, unhealthy into healthy tropics. English families have lived continuously in Barbados and Jamaica for between two and three centuries, proving that the British race can live and thrive in healthy tropics. It does not seem credible at present that the West Coast of Africa will ever be thus colonized, but it is already a different place from what it was forty years ago, largely because medical science is conquering malaria. Assuming that it can never be a home for British settlement, at least the economic results of medical science will be most marked. Administering, trading, developing, will be carried on without grievous loss of health and life, and without the consequent expense. The deadly lands will become scenes of everyday coming and going, not to be visited and left, but to be visited and returned to in safety and comfort.

The doctor in the past was called in to cure and to alleviate, by the individual rather than the State. He is now looked to, like the engineer and the water-bringer, to remove the obstacles which make against living in certain parts of the world. When Lord Lister died, *The Times* wrote, ' It is the drawback of so many discoveries and inventions that they take away from us almost as much as they give,' [1] and pointed out that no such drawback attached to the lifework of the great surgeon. What medical science is doing for the British Empire is wholly a gain. Outside the spiritual sphere it is the most purely beneficial agency that ever worked for the highest Imperial aims.

[1] February 17, 1912.

CHAPTER VI

THE INDIVIDUAL, THE COMPANY, AND THE STATE

It has been seen that the word Empire, and most of the words indicating parts of the British Empire, are of Roman origin. How far is that Empire itself in any sense of Roman origin? In other words, how far have the sources and methods of the British Empire been the sources and the methods which the Romans found and applied? The answer to the question is to be found by inquiring what part the individual and the State played in the two Empires respectively.

All great peoples and all Empires have had their great men, without whose agency they would not have been great; and personal influence and personal power were more to the front in old days than in our own; but the ordinary individual Roman played a smaller part in the making of the Roman Empire than the ordinary individual Englishman or Scotchman in the making of the British Empire. The British Empire is in the main an Anglo-Saxon creation, although its political nomenclature is Latin. In Mr. Heitland's *Roman Republic*, it is stated that the early Roman family 'was the groundwork of Roman life, for it is out of families, not of individuals, that the larger units, clan, tribe, State, were formed': that the family was under the absolute rule of the father; and that the power of the father in the family was the model for the Imperium.[1] Moreover, it has been seen that the dominant feature of the Roman Empire was that it was a military Empire. That is another way of saying that it was a creation of the State. The State may have been embodied, and more often than not was embodied, in a particular individual or in one or more particular leaders at a particular time, in Sulla or Julius Caesar or Augustus or Trajan; but it was the State with its political or military leaders, rather than the private individual, that was the moving force.

We are told that in the Roman Empire, at any rate in its early and prosperous times, 'to a degree now impossible commerce had the world in fee';[2] but it could not be maintained that the Roman Empire was created by commerce; on the contrary, commerce was created by the Roman Empire, by the pax Romana, the peace which was established by the strong hand of the Romans and their legionaries. The same writer tells us that 'trade from all parts of the Empire followed the eagles; merchants and soldiers were fellow pioneers.' Similarly Mr. Heitland writes: 'Even before the

[1] *The Roman Republic*, by W. G. Heitland, 1909, vol. i, chaps. vi and vii, pp. 35 and 39.

[2] Friedländer, authorized translation, vol. i, pp. 304, 312.

country was organized as a Province, traders (mercatores) were generally on the ground. Alleged ill-treatment of merchants was not seldom a pretext for campaigns and annexation.'[1] Mr. Arnold again says that 'The Roman trader was ubiquitous. He even preceded the Roman arms.'[2] Romans traded with nations and races outside their Empire. If Mithridates found 80,000 Italians to put to death in one day in the cities of Asia Minor, it must be assumed that not a few Roman or Italian traders had made their way beyond the actual limits of the Roman Province. In the days of Augustus a large fleet of Roman merchant vessels plied between the Red Sea and the Persian Gulf and India, diverting as far as possible the trade of the Far East from the land route through Persia to the ports of Egypt. But none the less it seems safe to say that, in the making of the Roman Empire, the Eagles usually went first; that the merchants, for the most part, came where—to use the terms of our own Empire—there was already a Roman Pretectorate or Roman sphere of influence; and that, so far as they contributed to the creation of the Empire, they did so by giving ground for further intervention in lands where the State through its soldiers had intervened already. 'The Romans were not an adventurous people'[3]: they

[1] *The Roman Republic*, vol. ii, p. 217.
[2] *Roman Provincial Administration*, p. 18.
[3] *Rome*, in the Home University Library series, p. 11, by W. Warde Fowler.

did not explore : they conquered : and their traders,
as a rule, waited till their soldiers had more or less
dominated the lands. In other words, they waited
for the State.

The Roman Empire began with conquest and
from first to last was mainly the result of expansion
by conquest. There was a centre, which centre
was a city, not a country, and which, being a city,
gave its colouring to the whole, making the Provinces
from the Roman point of view rather groups of
town communities than areas of country.[1] From
this centre, as already said, the Empire widened
out on all sides, always in continuity, by moving
frontiers outwards ; and almost always by conquest,
that is to say, by action of the State. The motive
forces of the Roman Empire were the instinct of
a military and conquering race, State policy and
material advantages, tribute for the Government
and the governing city, which meant relieving the
citizens of the governing city from the necessity
of paying taxes, and gain for the Roman merchants
and usurers who went out or sent out their
representatives into the Provinces.

The British Empire is not, and never was, the
London Empire. It never was the Empire of a city,
the Empire of a seat of Government. London is
the greatest city of the Empire ; but in overseas

---

[1] 'The Roman Empire was mainly an aggregate of cities which
were originally independent States.' Bury's *History of the Later
Roman Empire*, vol. i, p. 37.

enterprise, in early days, Bristol played a part as important as, or more important than, that played by London. What were the motives which led to the creation of the British Empire? Instinct, policy, material advantage, contributed to making it, as they contributed to making the Roman and every other Empire, but in very different forms and with widely different accompaniments. Conquest had nothing to do with the beginnings of the British Empire. The State at first played a very small part. The individual played a great part and led on the State. The Empire began with no continuity whatever, either of acquisition or of system. There was exploration, adventure, trade, and partial settlement which the Government licensed, disowned, or ignored at will, and which was all due to private initiative. There was little or nothing in the Roman Empire answering to the work of British explorers, adventurers, traders, and privateers in the sixteenth century, before England acquired any possession whatever overseas, with the exception of barren sovereignty over Newfoundland, or to the work of traders and colonizers of the seventeenth century.

The story of our Empire has been that British traders have always gone in front of the soldier and the State. They did not in old days content themselves with trading in Provinces which had been already made British or in which the strength of Britain had at least been felt and recognized. They traded and made footholds in foreign lands which became British in consequence of their trading. That has been pre-eminently the story of the English in India.

Religion has had much to say to the creation of the British Empire, and in a much greater degree as a personal influence than as part of a State policy. The missionary in our overseas records must be placed side by side with the trader as a pioneer of Empire. If it had not been for David Livingstone, for instance, it can hardly be supposed that we should now have the position which we have secured in Central Africa. Religious conviction again, or religious aversion, sent out British men and British families in numbers to settle overseas. For the Romans, on the other hand, and in the making of the Roman Empire, religion had little inspiring personal force. There was a State religion, but there was much more State than religion in it. ' It was the religion of the family, the religion also of the Empire of the world. Beginning in rustic simplicity, the traces of which it ever afterwards retained, it grew with the power of the Roman State, and became one with its laws. No fancy or poetry moulded the forms of the Roman gods; they are wanting in character and hardly distinguishable from one another. Not what they were, but their worship, is the point of interest about them. Those inanimate beings occasionally said a patriotic word at some critical juncture of the Roman affairs, but they had no attributes or qualities;

they are the mere impersonation of the needs of the State.' The Roman religion 'was truly the "established" religion. It represented the greatness and power of Rome.'[1] The Romans adopted other people's gods in addition to their own. Religious toleration was conspicuous among them, except when they saw political danger in a creed such as Judaism or Christianity; but their toleration was the toleration of indifference, and religion cannot be said to have been a living personal force to the Romans. Rome was not inspired to conquer by religion. Her conquests were not made in the name of and to the glory of the Roman gods. Nor did Roman pilgrim fathers go out to settle in strange lands. Christianity was the very opposite of the Roman religion. It made itself felt in the Roman Empire, as the religion of the individual not of the State, and thus, as Professor Bury points out, it operated as a dissolvent force in the Empire. It 'emphasized the privileges, hopes, and fears of the individual. Christ died for each man. It was thus opposed to the universality of the Roman world, in which the individual and his personal interests were of little account.'[2]

Over-population and consequent distress seems to have contributed to Roman as to British colonization, but the difference of the two cases is

---

[1] *Select passages from the Theological Writings of Benjamin Jowett* (1903), p. 163.

[2] Bury's *History of the Later Roman Empire*, vol. i, pp. 33-4.

very marked. The oversea colonies of Caius Gracchus were designed to relieve the over-population of Rome or Italy and find land for poor citizens. The colonies planted by Augustus had a similar intent, though, like most Roman colonies, they were largely composed of old soldiers. The Western half of the Empire could not have been so thoroughly Romanized, without a considerable amount of voluntary settlement of Romans and Italians in the Provinces, side by side with existing, or forming the nucleus of future colonies. But none the less the main feature of the Roman colonies was that they were part of a political machinery, whereby groups of Roman citizens were planted in conquered lands, holding in check existing communities which had come under the rule of Rome. In short, Roman colonization was in its essence a State matter.

British colonization, on the contrary, has in the main been independent of the State. Conquest and colonization have overlapped each other at certain periods in our overseas history, and in certain places, as in Canada; but, for the most part, the field of conquest has been distinct from the field of colonization. Gibbon Wakefield propounded a scheme of colonization, whereby the distribution of lands and the course of emigration were to be regulated by the State, and Lord Durham gave his high authority to the support of Wakefield's views; but those views never really took root, and British emigration as a whole went its way on the lines of the individual, not of the State. Now and again in the history of our Empire we find something that reminds us of Roman times and Roman ways, as when after the Crimean war the German legion was planted out in British Kaffraria and the eastern districts of the Cape Colony ; but if Roman and British colonization are set side by side, they differ on the whole, as town differs from country, as conquest differs from peaceful settlement, as the State differs from the individual man.

But, while the State was always in evidence in the Roman Empire, and while the individual rather than the State was the motive power in the British Empire, not only have there been eras in the British Empire when war was predominant and, therefore, the State, but also in many cases where and when the individual has been doing the work, some kind of sanction and of indirect support has come from the State.   The eighteenth century down to the Battle of Waterloo was what may be called the State era in the British Empire, the era *par excellence* of gain and loss by war and of the direct action of the State.   Canada, framed to be and proved to be a field of colonization, not a dependent Province, was secured not by British settlement but by war and by the State.   Australia, a field of colonization, the one great possession peacefully acquired in an era of war, was none the less acquired by the direct action of the State.   Moreover, when and where, in the making of the British Empire, the State has neither taken the initiative nor directly intervened, we can often trace indirect intervention, notably in the grant of Royal Charters to associations of private citizens.

The part played by the State and the individual in the Roman and the British Empires respectively can be well illustrated by considering and contrasting the position and the work of companies in the two Empires. Trading partnerships and companies are not peculiar to any race or any time, and among the Romans, as among other peoples, private citizens or associations of private citizens took contracts from the Government for the construction of public works or for other services, just as companies of contractors tender for and undertake the erection of public buildings, the building of ships, the supply of stores, the conveyance of mails and various public services at the present moment. It is stated that joint stock companies or syndicates first came into evidence in Roman history as doing work for the State, at the time of the Second Punic War, towards the end of the third century B.C., when they tendered for supplies to the Roman army in Spain;[1] but the companies of whom we hear most in connexion with the Roman State were the *Societates Publicanorum*, the companies of middlemen who farmed the tithes and other taxes in the later days of the Republic, and farmed some of the taxes under the Empire. Under the Republic they paid a lump sum

---

[1] Heitland's *Roman Republic*, vol. i, pp. 270, 351.

in each case to the Government and made what they could out of the taxpayers in the Provinces, being notorious as machinery for extortion and misgovernment. The members of these companies were capitalists, belonging exclusively or almost exclusively to one particular class of Roman citizens. Thus it may be said that in the Roman system, companies, so far as they had to do with the State and the Empire, were purely private companies, but were most in evidence as undertaking by contract one of the principal functions of the State, the collection of revenue. They were private citizens who were middlemen and monopolists of State revenues, who did not produce or create directly or indirectly for the State, but who took over purely State work as a matter of speculation. Their existence and their functions seem to point to the fact that the Romans, if State led, were, at the same time, by no means State ridden. In modern days State intervention is accompanied by multiplication of officials, whereas in lieu of creating a regular Civil Service to collect their revenues, the Romans, at any rate in the earlier days of Roman rule, left the duty to private contractors.

There does not seem to be any parallel in the British Empire to these companies of *publicani*. On the other hand, there is no parallel in the Roman Empire to the chartered companies, who have played such a notable part in our own Empire. In a sense these companies have been middlemen and monopolists, that is to say, they have been a kind of inter-

mediate agency, really doing State work, and in
their original guise in past centuries they held
a trading monopoly from the State as against other
British citizens.   The great East India Company
held a licence or charter from the Crown to carry
on trade in certain lands and waters to the exclusion
of other British traders.   But the shareholders in
the East India Company and in other British chartered companies were not concerned with exploiting
lands which had already been thoroughly conquered
and dominated by Great Britain, nor with speculating
in revenues which accrued to the British Government, but with trading in lands wholly outside
British rule or colonizing lands which were at most
only British in name.   They held no contracts from
the Government, only a licence from the Government and a safeguard against competition from
home.   They took the whole risk.   They made no
profit out of the State, but indirectly brought profit
to the State.   A *Societas Publicanorum* was a purely
private company, not incorporated by the State, but
it did absolutely nothing but speculate in State work
in countries which belonged to the State.   The East
India Company was not a purely private company,
in that it was incorporated by the State, but it
embodied private British commercial enterprise.   It
illustrated the initiative of private British citizens,
who went in front of the State and played a conspicuous part in building up the British Empire.
Roman citizens never seem to have formed associa-

tions of this kind and on these lines. They did work for the State and made profit out of the State, but they took their lead from, rather than gave the lead to, the State; and they did not to any appreciable degree go outside and beyond the State.

The merits and demerits of chartered companies have often been discussed. Whatever may be said for or against them, the fact remains that the British Empire, as it stands to-day, is in no small degree the outcome of chartered companies, which have been a machinery peculiarly adapted to the British type. There are three points in this connexion which it may be well to emphasize, that chartered companies have been of different degrees and kinds, that there have been two distinct eras of chartered companies in the British Empire, and that these companies have been of rather special value to that Empire as contributing a much needed element of continuity.

The Spaniards and Portuguese did not make much use of chartered companies for their overseas work; though comparatively late in their history, in the middle of the seventeenth century, the Portuguese, under pressure of war with the Dutch in Brazil, took a leaf out of their enemy's book and established a Brazil company; while a century later, the Portuguese minister, Pombal, created similar companies, also in connexion with Brazil. The French used chartered companies, but the genius of France did not lie in this direction. French chartered companies were not so much the outcome of commercial initiative from below as the creations of the State from above; and in France the State was the King and his particular Minister for the time being, Richelieu in one reign, Colbert in another. The French companies, therefore, wanted vitality, they suffered from constant interference by the Government and were perpetually made and unmade. The Northern—the Teuton and Scandinavian—peoples, especially the Dutch and the English, were most successful in their chartered companies. The two great Dutch chartered companies, the East India Company and the West India Company, practically embodied the State in its overseas dealings. They were national associations rather than private concerns. The British chartered companies, on the other hand, were private concerns rather than national associations; but they did national work. The influence of the State in connexion with chartered companies was far more felt in France and in the Netherlands than in England. In France it worked against strength and continuity, and killed the usefulness of the companies. In the Netherlands it gave such wholesale and continuous support to the companies that they were practically identified with the State. In England the Government was not so pernicious to the companies as in France, and gave no such unwavering support to them as in Holland. The British chartered companies remained private companies.

As the historic British chartered companies differed from the chartered companies of other nations in being less closely connected with the State or less constantly interfered with by the State, so the later British chartered companies have differed from the old chartered companies. The old chartered companies, which contributed so greatly to the making of the British Empire, may be said to have come to an end, at any rate in their Empire-making capacity, when the Government of India was taken over by the Crown from the East India Company in 1858, and when the Hudson Bay Company in 1869 surrendered their territorial rights to the Canadian Government. But within a very few years from this date a new series of chartered companies came into existence, for between 1880 and 1890 the British North Borneo Company, the Royal Niger Company, the Imperial British East Africa Company, and the British South Africa Company, all received charters from the Crown ; and through their agency, directly or indirectly, little short of a new Empire came into existence. It is one of the most interesting features in the record of the British Empire, that its latest developments have been accompanied by and largely accomplished through the agencies which did so much for the original beginnings of the Empire. Once more in British history the individual led the State, and the State worked through and gave some endorsement to the individual. The first of these latter-day chartered companies, still in vigorous operation, was the British North Borneo Company, which received its charter in 1881. The founders of the company had already acquired a large extent of territory from native Sultans, but in granting the charter, the Crown assumed no Dominion or sovereignty over the territories so acquired—such as would have been assumed under the old charters, and instead of giving to the company in their sphere of action a general monopoly of trade, it expressly prohibited any such general monopoly. Thus the new type of charter differed from the old type in that the State disclaimed sovereign rights over territorial acquisitions made by its subjects, thereby holding itself even more aloof than before from the responsibilities which the private citizens incurred ; and, on the other hand, it restricted the trading monopoly which had been the mainspring of the old companies so as to ensure that individual citizens, other than shareholders of the company, should trade at will with the territories which the company had acquired.   In either respect the new type of charter tended to encourage private initiative.[1]

The weakest point in British colonial policy, taken as a whole, has been want of continuity. Most of our mistakes and misfortunes, notably in the past history of South Africa, have arisen from this cause. Writing of the state of feeling in Upper Canada at

---

[1] For a comparison of the old and the new charters reference should be made to Lord Granville's dispatch to Sir R. Morier of January 7, 1882, printed in Blue Book C. 3108, 1882.

the time of his mission, Lord Durham said in his report, ' They ask for greater firmness of purpose in their rulers, and a more defined and consistent policy on the part of the Government; something, in short, that will make all parties feel that an order of things has been established, to which it is necessary that they should conform themselves, and which is not to be subject to any unlooked for and sudden inter-ruption, consequent upon some unforeseen move in the game of politics in England.' [1]   In this respect the Romans were infinitely superior to the English. They had a defined and consistent policy, and established an order of things to which all peoples in their Empire felt that they must conform them-selves.   This is the good side of State omnipotence, as opposed to individual freedom and initiative. Individual freedom has made itself felt in bringing about party government in England; and, so far as party government has affected Imperial policy, its influence has been all for the bad because it has been all against continuity.   It has been stated above that in the beginnings of the British Empire there was no continuity and no system.   This was in the seventeenth century, when the great Civil War took place and when State authority was constantly changing and much at a discount.   But this same age was also a notable age for chartered companies, and chartered companies in their work beyond the seas in no small degree supplied the continuity

[1] 1912 ed., vol. ii, p. 192.

which the State did not give, for they held under the
Government for the time being, whether it was this
king or that king, or king or Parliament, and so far as
their individual members did not compromise them,
they had nothing to do with one party rather than
another. Being chartered companies they had public
recognition at home and abroad, being composed of
private merchants they did not stand or fall with
this or that Government or party. In the seventeenth century very especially, but also in later ages
and in our own times, these companies have conspicuously contributed to continuity. For this we
owe them a debt of gratitude, as also for the scope
which they have given for evolving a race of
administrators out of trading surroundings which led
on to conquest and to rule.

If the private British citizen, either alone or in
combination, has taken a great part in making the
Empire, he has a great part to play in keeping it.
Empires necessarily imply inclusion of different
races and different types of the same race. In all
Empires individuals must have great indirect influence. The individual Briton or German or Dacian
or Numidian must have formed a liking or a hatred
for the Romans as a whole, largely from the kind of
individual Roman with whom he came into contact,
just as the native of India must inevitably judge of
the British people as a whole from the individual
Englishmen whom he has served or whom he has
met. But the less an Empire depends upon force of

arms, the more it depends for cohesion upon individual characteristics, and in this respect, as in others, the individual is of more importance in the British than in the Roman Empire. He is perhaps of most importance in that half of the Empire from which the element of force has been most eliminated, that is, in regard to the relations between the Self-Governing Dominions and the Mother Country. State wisdom or unwisdom may do much to make or mar good relations, but a more potent force still, and growing in potency as the opportunities of meeting multiply owing to better communication, is the action and reaction of individual citizens. This point has already been referred to in a previous chapter in connexion with the subject of old and young peoples. It is impossible to exaggerate the good which can be done by individuals and associations of individuals, such as the Victoria League, which bear in mind the individual from over the seas. For an Empire is a collection of human beings who live individual and private lives, and it will never be made one or remain one, unless public ties are supplemented by private intimacy and friendship, and unless to the sense of common citizenship is added the sure feeling of welcome to the family and the home.

CHAPTER VII

CLASS, COLOUR, AND RACE

THE main differences between ancient and modern political systems are usually held to be, that in the ancient world representative institutions were unknown, and that slavery was a fundamental element in every ancient community. Negro slavery and the slave trade have stained the records of the British Empire: but only in certain tropical dependencies of Great Britain—mainly the West Indies—was slavery ever in any sense an integral factor. In the Roman Empire, on the other hand, it was a standing and universal institution; and the existence of slavery throughout that Empire created a great class distinction between freemen and slaves, which was both political and social, and which neither has nor ever had any counterpart in the British Empire. Under the conditions of the old world, slavery was not inimical to Empire; and in the Roman Empire it was not altogether a source of weakness and danger. Mr. Arnold states that, with the extension of the citizenship, 'the Roman Empire came to be a homogeneous mass of privileged persons';[1] and it may fairly be argued that the existence of slavery

[1] *Roman Provincial Administration*, p. 42.

tended to produce this result, and to create a bond among all those within the Empire who were not slaves, as being privileged persons, which bond counteracted differences of race. The Roman Empire was a military despotism evolved out of a Republic or an oligarchy which had ceased to meet the requirements of the time. Slavery harmonized with despotism; it was in a sense an appropriate base of the pyramid; slaves and freemen alike were of various races and colours; and the result of slavery in the Roman Empire was to make a class distinction which not only did not follow but tended to obliterate the lines of race.

Among the freemen of the Roman Empire how far did class operate? What relation did it bear to race? and how far can we find parallels in our own Empire?

It is very difficult to compare Roman and British citizenship, or, as has been shown by a recent discussion in the pages of *United Empire*, to define exactly what British citizenship means. Citizenship among the Greeks and Romans attached to the persons, not to the place where they lived. The State was a collection of citizens, not a territory; for the earliest basis of political community, as Sir Henry Maine has pointed out, was kinship in blood, not local contiguity.[1] Full Roman citizenship included both public and private rights, the former consisting of the franchise and eligibility to office in

[1] *Ancient Law*, chap. v.

the State, the latter embodying, among other
privileges, exemption from what amounted to
martial law. 'The martial law under which all
other provincials lay, did not apply to him who could
say with St. Paul, "I am a Roman."' [1] In the early
days of Rome there was a great gulf fixed between
the citizen and the non-citizen, between the *civis*
and the *peregrinus*, and though citizenship did not
attach to the soil, it is interesting to notice that land
within the boundaries of the old Roman State was
held by a specially privileged tenure in Roman law,
which was afterwards extended to most of the soil of
Italy, but not to the Provinces. As Roman power
widened in Italy, different shades of partial citizenship came into existence ; private rights, all or
some, were given to individuals; public rights, all or
some, were given to town communities. Then the
full Roman citizenship was extended to Italy ; and
finally, at the beginning of the third century A.D., it
was made universal throughout the Empire. From
this time the only distinction left was that between
freemen and slaves. It will be noted that the more
Roman citizenship extended beyond the city walls,
the less valuable one element in it, the franchise,
became ; for, as the Romans had no representative
institutions, a Roman citizen could only vote by
going to Rome, and when the Republic was ex-
changed for a despotism the vote at Rome became of
little value.

[1] Arnold's *Roman Provincial Administration*, pp. 71-2.

Starting originally with the tie of race as the basis of citizenship, the Romans stand out beyond almost all peoples in the extent to which they disregarded race, and in the liberality with which they widened their citizenship.   Here is Bacon's verdict upon them:

'Never any State was in this point so open to receive strangers into their body as were the Romans. Therefore, it sorted with them accordingly; for they grew to the greatest monarchy.   Their manner was to grant naturalization (which they called *jus civitatis*), and to grant it in the highest degree; that is not only *jus commercii*, *jus connubii*, *jus hereditatis*, but also *jus suffragii* and *jus honorum*.   And this not to singular persons alone, but likewise to whole families; yea, to cities, and sometimes to nations.   Add to this their custom of plantation of colonies, whereby the Roman plant was removed into the soil of other nations.   And putting both constitutions together, you will say that it was not the Romans that spread upon the world, but it was the world that spread upon the Romans; and that was the sure way of greatness.' [1]

Emphasis has been laid in the preceding pages upon the military basis of the Roman Empire; but that Empire was, it need hardly be said, infinitely more than a mere creation of brute force.   Gibbon calls the story of Rome 'the rise of a city, which swelled into an Empire'.[2]   And in truth the Romans

---

[1] 'Of the true greatness of Kingdoms and Estates,' Spedding's edition, vol. vi, p. 448.

[2] General observations on the Fall of the Roman Empire in the West (*Decline and Fall*, 1862 ed., vol. iv, p. 403).

were the one people in the history of the world who gradually and surely expanded a town into a world-wide community. With singular breadth of view and practical statesmanship, they widened the city State by extending the privileges of the walled city of Rome to individuals and peoples whom the city and its citizens had conquered. Their great invention in politics was universal citizenship developed out of the citizenship of one—the greatest among many cities; and we owe to them municipal government in the modern sense, in that they created a combination of limited local self-government with the wider Imperial status which originally attached only to the central city, Rome.

Now what does British citizenship amount to? The inhabitants of all territories which have been formally annexed by Great Britain are British subjects, and are entitled to all the privileges which British subjects can claim as against foreigners. They are *cives* as against *peregrini*; and their privileges attach to them in virtue of being natives of British soil. But the British Empire includes large territories which have not been annexed and are not British soil. They are British Protectorates, and the natives of these Protectorates are not in the eye of the law British subjects. These British Protectorates seem to be somewhat analogous to the *civitates foederatae* in the earlier days of Roman history, before all political distinctions were swept away. Naturalization again is not as yet on one and the same basis for the whole Empire; though it must be noted that when Bacon, in the passage which has been quoted, speaks of Roman naturalization, he means in effect the raising of Roman subjects into full Roman citizens, whereas British naturalization means the conversion of foreign subjects or aliens into British subjects. The result of the discussion on naturalization at the last Imperial Conference was to make a further advance towards uniformity in naturalization throughout the British Empire; but still, at the present time, a man may be naturalized in Canada under the Dominion Laws and become a British citizen in Canada, while, if he moves within a certain time to some other part of the British Empire, he ceases to be a British citizen. Nor is there any uniform franchise for the whole Empire, inasmuch as though there is an Imperial Government, there is not, as in the Roman Empire, one Government and one only. British subjects in India are *cives sine suffragio*; and while British subjects in Canada have the *jus suffragii*, it is not a vote for the whole Empire. Nor once more have all British subjects the full *jus honorum*. For instance, there is a remnant of religious disabilities in that a Roman Catholic cannot be Lord Chancellor of England. Race disqualification, though very rare under the Imperial Government, is illustrated by the fact that candidates for the Civil Service of the Far Eastern colonies must be natural born British subjects of pure European descent; and it may be presumed that some of the highest posts in the Empire would in fact be reserved for white men.

The greatest difficulty in the British Empire is probably the colour question. It has been already pointed out that this colour question appears to be a modern problem. There is little reference to it in Roman writers. The Romans were not called upon to deal with large numbers of coloured races. The alien peoples with whom they were brought into contact, or whom they ruled, were usually of the same colour as themselves; and when and where they did govern coloured peoples, there is no evidence that colour, *quâ* colour, created any special barrier between rulers and ruled.

There was no doubt strong race feeling among the Romans for the West as against the East. The Western half of the Empire was Romanized. The Eastern half was Hellenized. The Roman model was followed, Roman *coloniae* and *municipia* were multiplied, to a greater extent in the West than in the East; and the Romans drew their leaders and their officials far more from the Western Provinces than from Egypt or Asia. But the feeling or prejudice does not seem to have been primarily based on colour. Northern Africa to the west of Egypt and Cyrenaica was in the Western sphere. Egypt was in the Eastern. Colour must have been as much in evidence in Mauretania as in Egypt, but there was a race instinct among the Romans against Egypt and its ways which did not apply to the Romanized districts of North Africa further West.

Nor again, as has been said, was slavery in the Roman Empire in any way based on colour; and it is probably to this fact, as contrasted with the fact that in modern times a special coloured race— the Negro race—was marked out for slavery in the overseas possessions of European nations, that the difference of feeling on the subject of colour in Roman times and in our own should be attributed. Or possibly it should be traced more especially to the time of abolition of slavery and the consequent equalizing of the white and black races in the eyes of the law. Slave emancipation intensified with apprehension the colour feeling of the white oligarchy in the lands where slavery had prevailed, and it may well be that those lands became a nucleus whence colour prejudice spread outside the former areas of negro slavery, and coalesced, for instance, with the feeling of West as against East, in which, far more than was the case in the Roman Empire, the element of colour is also present.[1] In the Self-Governing Provinces of the British Empire at the present day the coloured natives of the soil, though British subjects, are, more often than not, excluded from the franchise, as in Australia, for instance, or parts of South Africa, or British Columbia; while

---

[1] On the subject of the colour question in ancient and modern times see Lord Cromer's *Ancient and Modern Imperialism*. The views which he has expressed seem to be generally accepted.

in New Zealand, the Maoris have a special representation ; and most, if not all, of the Self-Governing
Dominions have laws designed to restrict the
admission of coloured immigrants, whether they
are British subjects or whether they are not. In
other words, in the British Empire there are
disabilities attaching to race and colour, which
found no place in the Roman Empire.

It should be noted, however, with regard to the
colour question, so far as it concerns the relations
between England and her dependencies at the
present day, that the feeling on the subject is not
merely the result of prejudice, but the result also of
practical experience. In other words, colour prejudice is one thing, and what may be called colour
discrimination is another. The white man may be,
and usually is, prejudiced against the coloured man,
because he himself is white, while the other is
coloured ; and the prejudice is probably mutual.
But the white man, or at any rate the Englishman,
also finds more rational ground for discrimination,
in that the qualities, character, and upbringing of
most coloured men are not those which are in
demand for a ruling race, and are not, except in
rare individual cases, eliminated by education on
the white man's lines. The same discrimination is
made by coloured races themselves, or some of them.
A peasant in India would, speaking generally, look
for justice to an Englishman in preference to one
of his own race, and if a coloured race has to

submit to alien rule, the white man's rule would probably be preferred to that of coloured men who are foreign to the soil. It is one thing for natives of India to be placed in authority in their own land and over their own countrymen; it is another for them to be placed in authority over Malays, Chinese, or any of the African and Pacific races, and vice versa. Hence the system of open competition, as applied to an Empire of multifarious races, like our own, presents obvious difficulties and needs to be safeguarded. Had the Romans extended their rule into tropical Africa or Farther Asia, we might have heard more of the colour question in their Empire; and, as it was, though they took little account of different shades of colour, they practically drew upon the West for the government of the East on much the same principle that we look to our own white race for the administration of the tropics.

It may be summed up that in the Roman Empire there was a perpetual opening out of citizenship. The tendency was all towards fusion and uniformity, and race imposed few or no barriers. In the British Empire we have started with British citizenship of one kind or another as coterminous with British soil, in whatever part of the world the soil may be; but the tendency has been to greater diversity rather than to greater uniformity; and the lessening of distance has accentuated, instead of obliterating, distinctions of race. But at the same time it must be borne in mind that the grant of universal citizenship in the Roman Empire was combined with the stereotyping of military despotism. It would be perhaps more accurate to say that all Roman citizens became lowered to the level of Roman subjects, than that all Roman subjects were raised to the level of Roman citizens. Equality came in the Roman Empire as the result of the loss of freedom. Diversity has developed in the British Empire as the result of the growth of freedom. The race and colour problem has increased in difficulty in our Empire in proportion as some of the Provinces of that Empire have become more and more self-governing, as the Empire has developed into two Empires, of which more will be said in a later chapter.

Leaving the question of citizenship, let us now ask what class distinctions in the ordinary sense there were among the citizens of the Roman Empire, and how far they corresponded to our own. There were rich and poor, then as always, very rich and very poor, millionaires and paupers as in our own day, and as the Empire went on towards decay, luxury and extravagance increased in the upper classes—a warning to ourselves. There were old Patrician families and *nouveaux riches*, and a class which has no parallel at the present day, of freedmen whose former masters became their patrons with certain rights by law or custom. There were privileges and disabilities attaching to particular

classes. Senators had various privileges, and from
the time of Augustus there was a hereditary
senatorial class, analogous to the peers in the
United Kingdom, though the eldest son of a
senator did not *ipso facto* have on his father's death
a seat in the Senate. Senators, on the other hand,
incurred disabilities. For instance, they were de-
barred by law and custom from taking a direct
part in money-lending and financial business, and
this business was almost exclusively in the hands
of another class, the Equites. In the later stages of
the Empire, social position seems to have been
mainly determined by Government employment.
'The aristocracy of the Roman Empire in the
fifth century was an aristocracy of officials. This is
a fact to be borne in mind, that social rank ultimately
depended upon a public career.'[1] In earlier days it
may be assumed that, while bureaucracy was on the
increase, social distinctions were, on the whole,
much the same among Romans as among us;
but we look in vain in the Roman Empire for a
counterpart to the growing strength and importance of labour in modern society and in modern
politics, and the development of a Labour Party or
parties.

---

[1] Bury's *History of the Later Roman Empire*, vol. i, pp. 38-9. The
writer points out that the members of the senatorial class were
wholly removed from local or municipal surroundings, that 'the
senatorial world was thus the undiluted atmosphere of pure Roman
Imperialism', and that the Empire came to consist of the Emperor,
the senators, and the mass of Roman citizens.

Manual labour among the Romans was, under the Republic and at the beginning of the Empire, almost exclusively slave labour. 'The slave class of antiquity really corresponded to our free labouring class.'[1] The Roman plebs, who demanded *panem et Circenses*, did not apparently consist of wage-earners. They were rather a privileged class of unemployed, who looked to the State and to the conquests made by the State to keep them fed and amused. This fact, that manual labour was in the main slave labour, accounts for the absence of any definite labour movement or labour problems in the Roman Empire, as apart from the general question of poverty. We do not read of questions as to rates of wages and hours of work playing any appreciable part in the story of Rome and the Roman Empire, presumably for the reason that so many of the workmen were not citizens but chattels. In our own Empire where white workers and coloured workers are side by side, as in South Africa, it would be fair to say that they do not work on the same level, and that the white man is rather the overseer of, than the fellow-workman with, the coloured man. But notwithstanding, wherever both coloured men and white men are free agents, the element of labour competition enters in ; and where, as in Australia, the land is by nature adapted to be a white man's land and at the

---

[1] Dill's *Roman Society from Nero to Marcus Aurelius*, 2nd ed., 1905, Bk. I, chap. iii, 'The Society of the Freedmen,' p. 102.

same time the indigenous coloured men are not numerous, the tendency to exclude coloured labour is largely due to the white labourer's determination not to allow his labour to be undersold and his wages to be reduced by the incoming of cheaper coloured labour.   Where slavery was in existence, no such element of competition could arise, for even if skilled slaves were wage-earners, they were not in a position to determine upon what terms they would sell their labour.[1]

Mr. Dill tells us that under the Empire a numerous and important class of freedmen grew up and brought into the State the element, which had not previously existed, of free industrial labour.   The different trades had their clubs and societies, somewhat resembling modern Trades Unions, but being rather combinations for social purposes than for the protection of wage-earners against the capitalists.[2] If, however, free industrial labour on a considerable scale came into existence, it does not seem to have produced any of the political and economic developments which have attended the modern labour movement.   Presumably, to the end, the proportion of slaves among the labourers was large, and among

[1] For the extent to which at Athens (whatever may have been the case at Rome) slave artisans and free artisans were 'fellow-workers', see Mr. Zimmern's *Greek Commonwealth* (1911).

[2] In addition to what Mr. Dill tells us as to these Guilds or Clubs, see Mr. Warde Fowler's *Rome* in the Home University Library Series, pp. 223-5.   The guilds seem to have been largely what would now be called funeral clubs.   Mr. Fowler says that we do not hear much of slave labour in the provincial towns of the Roman Empire.

the free labourers a considerable proportion were freedmen, men who had been slaves, who still owed a kind of allegiance to their former masters, and who being themselves placed in a privileged position by the fact of having been given their freedom, were not one in feeling with the whole multitude of manual labourers. To use a modern term, there was no solidarity in the labour movement in the Roman Empire, if there ever was any labour movement at all; and labour was prevented from forming one class by being itself divided into the two great classes of slave and free.

In our own days the labour movement attracts universal attention in the political and industrial world. The Liberalism of the last century in this country, from the date of the great Reform Bill onwards, directed its energies to curtailing class privileges and working for common citizenship and equality of chances. The aim was a noble one; the dream was gradually to wipe out class distinctions in the State, so that the State should all be one. But, as democracy grew in strength, and more especially as it developed in the younger nations of the British Empire where custom and tradition had not the same binding force as in the older land, class reappeared from below and became far more than ever a political as well as an industrial basis. Thus what had been regarded as an evil half a century ago has now become, for the time being at any rate, a settled principle of politics; and a Labour Party, that is, a political combination based exclusively and avowedly on class feeling and class interests, is a prominent feature, perhaps the most prominent feature, in the public life of our time. How far does this great revival or new assertion of class accord with or militate against the instinct of race, and what bearing has it upon the future of the Empire?

The existence of a Labour Party implies the growing claims to ascendancy of manual labour; it is a pronouncement that manual labour has a right not only to safeguard its own interests, but to bid for and in the name of the majority to acquire the control of the State. The Australian Labour Party govern the Commonwealth of Australia at the present time. They govern it as being Australians, that is, as residents in or citizens of a certain country, and as being representatives of labour, that is, of a class. Other Governments in plenty have governed in fact as representatives of some privileged class; but in the case of a Labour Government and a Labour Party, class is openly inscribed on the banner. Now class is not coterminous with a particular race or confined by the limits of any particular country or Empire. We have seen that in the Roman system, the existence of slavery, that is, of class distinction in its most violent form, tended to modify and in large measure counteract distinction of race. What are the relations of class to race under modern conditions, class having become the fundamental basis of one great political party? The answer is that the lines of class largely coincide with the lines of race, so far as the lines of race coincide with the lines of colour. The labour movement, as it exists in the Self-Governing Dominions, is beyond question closely allied to the feeling of white against coloured races. Race affinity prefers the white man to the coloured man ; class interest militates against the Indian or Chinese labourer as willing and able to work for less money than the white workman. From this it follows that in the British Empire the tie of class runs counter to the tie of citizenship. To the labour man in Australasia it is of little or no account that an incoming coloured workman is a British subject, if he comes from India. He is a coloured man, not a white man, and a more dangerous competitor in the wage market than a white labourer, because his conditions of life and terms of work are not the white man's conditions and terms. We have then, as against the great fundamental class distinction in the Roman Empire between freemen and slaves, which was not based on race, a great fundamental distinction in the British Empire which is based on race, and which class interest has adopted and accentuated.

But when we leave the colour question out of sight, and deal only with white men, how far do class and race coincide? The answer is that the tie of class runs counter, if not to the tie of race, at least to the tie of nationality. It is one of the problems of the future, whether the labour man in a British land will be found in line with the labour man in a non-British land, as against the capitalist class similarly combined in the two countries, or whether the labour man and the capitalist alike will be British citizens first and labour men and capitalists respectively only in the second place. So far as class feeling and class interest predominates, it is an influence working directly against the tie of nationality and citizenship of Empire. Problems of this kind did not greatly trouble the Roman Empire, for the simple reason that they are the fruits of freedom. The Roman Empire ultimately meant the Roman legions. As time went on, the different legions no doubt represented to a large extent different races, the West or the North or the East, but military despotism and the existence of slavery accounted between them for the absence of the conflicting tendencies which make the present history of our own Empire at once so perplexing and so full of interest.

It may be conjectured and hoped that the race instinct in the British Empire, more natural, less associated with material gains than the bond of class, will in the end prove the stronger force among the white citizens of the Empire. But there are cases in which this class tie has peculiar danger in the eyes of those who are concerned for the future of the Empire. The Trades Unions in Canada are in great measure affiliated to the Trades Unions in the United States, and the chief centres of the Unions are in most cases in the United States. Here we have two neighbouring countries, one part of the British Empire, the other not, and the country which belongs to the British Empire in no small degree peopled from the United States. We have kinship in race, language, and tradition, though not in nationality; and consequently here, in a unique and unusual degree, the tie of class coincides with the tie of race and, therefore, is a peculiarly strong factor as against the tie of citizenship or nationality.

This instance of Canada and of Trades Unions in Canada with their connexions in the United States suggests that, in a chapter dealing with class, colour, and race, a point well worth attention by those who are trying to forecast our future, is the question: What will be the political relations in the coming time between the British Empire and the United States? The question may well be asked, because as a matter of fact one great Province of the Empire, Canada, destined in the judgement of many well able to judge to be the corner stone of the arch of the Empire, has had its whole history moulded by the proximity of the United States, and also because the British future seems likely to shape itself in an increasingly closer connexion with the United States. There comes, therefore, upon the screen a rival picture to the British Empire in the form of some kind or other of Anglo-Saxon Federation. A rival picture it is, or would probably be, because it is difficult to believe that a federation of the kind would not be a dissolvent of Empire. The younger nations of the present Empire, if brought into some kind of partnership with the great Republic— already, in its own comparative youthfulness and surpassing strength, a most powerful attraction to growing peoples—would tend to become independent members of a loosely bound political system, in lieu of being, as at present, integral parts of an Empire under what Lord Durham well called, 'the stable authority of a hereditary monarchy';[1] and the new organization, having its root in race affinity, would militate against the Empire citizenship which takes no count of race. It is an alluring dream of what is probably impracticable, but which finds some substantial backing in the class connexions to which reference has been made. The whole basis of any scheme of the kind would be race affinity, but as the years have gone on, race affinity between England and the United States has become more and more alloyed by the enormous influx into the American Republic of immigrants not of British and very largely not of Teuton stock. The Americans, too, have in abundance race and colour problems of their own, and it is difficult to picture any time, however distant, at which they would welcome any kind of close combination with an Empire full of

[1] 1912 ed., vol. ii, p. 263.

race and colour problems. Growing friendship between Great Britain and the British Dominions on the one hand, and the United States on the other, we all desire ; but a sober outlook for the future stops at that point, and reserves to the British Empire an undivided destiny.

CHAPTER VIII

THE NATURAL AND THE ARTIFICIAL

DURING the era in England which began with the great Reform Bill, included the triumph of Free Trade, and lasted more or less until the nineteenth century was drawing towards its close, there was in politics and economics what may be called a standard creed, which was more especially the creed of the Whigs, and their successors, the old-time Liberals. This creed was that artificial restrictions should as far as possible be removed, that natural forces are the healthy forces and should be given full play, that State interference should be rare, and that State activity should be directed rather towards repealing old laws than to making new ones. It was a creed which had a most sound basis, because it harmonized with the English instinct in favour of individual initiative, but, being carried too far, it brought inevitable reaction.

The wholehearted professors and adherents of this creed held that the colonies should govern themselves, frame their own tariffs, undertake their own defence, do what they pleased, and shape their own futures. If they declared for independence, such a finale, it was held, would be only logical and according to nature. British emigrants should go where

they pleased, to British colonies or to foreign countries indifferently, because they knew their own
business best, and their movement should not be
guided by anything but individual interests. ' Force
is no remedy' was a favourite phrase, applied more
especially in connexion with Ireland, and meaning
that the hand of man is in the long run powerless
as against the forces of nature. Considering how
strongly these views were held, and how often they
are in one form or another still called upon to do
duty, when one party or another finds it expedient
to appeal to the old faith, it is worth while to ask
the question how far the artificial as opposed to the
natural has been in evidence in the Roman and the
British Empires respectively.

Everything made by man is artificial, whether it is
a building or an institution or an Empire. A state of
nature is an unclothed world. But how far, we ask,
does the history of the Roman Empire or of the
British Empire bear out the dictum that force is no
remedy, that no human system can be permanent
which is not based upon but in a greater or less
degree runs counter to nature? If you wait long
enough, everything human in time decays, and the
argument can always be used that it would not have
decayed if it had not been artificial. This is the
kind of judgement which is so often passed upon
the Roman Empire. People need to be reminded
of the very carefully weighed words in which Gibbon
refers to the fall of the Roman Empire in the West.

'The decline of Rome was the natural and inevitable effect of immoderate greatness. Prosperity ripened the principle of decay; the causes of destruction multiplied with the extent of conquest; and as soon as time or accident had removed the artificial supports, the stupendous fabric yielded to the pressure of its own weight. The story of its ruin is simple and obvious; and instead of inquiring why the Roman Empire was destroyed, we should rather be surprised that it subsisted so long.'[1]

These words of Gibbon may be taken either as pointing out that the Roman Empire fell because it was an artificial structure and exceeded natural limits, or as emphasizing the strength which an artificial creation attained. The great difficulty in the case of the Roman Empire is to choose any even approximate dates when it may be said to have begun and when it may be said to have ended. Mr. Arnold, at the beginning of his work on Roman Provincial Administration, lays down that, 'Taking the terms in their widest extent, the Roman Provincial Administration may be said to have lasted for some 700 years, from the final settlement of Sicily after the second Punic war to the apparent destruction of the system by the barbarians,'[2] that is until the fall of what is commonly known as the Western Empire in A.D. 476. At least, he gives to the Provincial Administration a

---

[1] *Decline and Fall*, 1862 ed., vol. iv, p. 403: 'General Observations on the Fall of the Roman Empire in the West.'

[2] *Roman Provincial Administration*, p. 1.

life of 500 years. The Eastern Empire or the Eastern half of the Empire long outlived the Western half and, in Freeman's words, 'Kept the political tradition of the elder Empire unbroken.'[1] However we look at it, the Roman Empire, in one form or another, was very long-lived, and side by side with its long life, we have to set the fact that it was a most artificial creation, the one artificial creation which placed itself beyond all competition and became coterminous with the civilized world. It was based on force, and it stands out to all time as contradicting the dictum that force is no remedy. At the same time, while the Roman Empire was essentially artificial, it made what may be called concessions to nature. Though differences of race and nationality were in the main overridden or ignored, the great root difference between East and West was recognized, and the East was left to be Greek in civilization rather than Roman. Though the Empire was the result of conquest, the conquest was to a large extent the result of natural expansion. The Empire grew by constant and continuous accretions of adjoining territory, not by acquisition of lands wholly removed from the centre of life. Further, with some exceptions, such as Britain and Dacia, there were more or less natural boundaries to the Empire, which were more or less observed, the ocean, the desert on the south, the great rivers of the Rhine, the Danube, and the Euphrates. Within the Empire, too, in

---

[1] *Historical Geography of Europe*, 1882 ed., p. 375.

Mr. Arnold's words, 'the Romans showed greater power of assimilation than has been shown by any other conquerors,' and they 'were not cursed with the passion for uniformity.'[1] They actively encouraged municipal institutions, they tolerated local creeds, their armed forces gave peace, and peace made for natural conditions under a military despotism, which was an artificial régime.

In a previous chapter it has been attempted to show that the British Empire has owed more to the initiative of private individual citizens and less to the State than was the case with the Roman Empire. That is another way of saying that our own Empire is not such an artificial handiwork as was the Roman Empire. Inconsistent, illogical, full of contradictions and diversities, the British Empire gives every evidence of having in great measure grown at will, as opposed to being made to order. Men argue, therefore, looking at this Empire and considering how it has come into existence, that what is lasting is based on nature, and what is transient is the outcome of State interference and human will or caprice. To illustrate how dangerous generalizations of this kind are, we will take the case of one great Province of the British Empire, Canada, and examine how far Canada of to-day is a natural or an artificial creation.

Canada was first colonized by the French. Its beginnings were, in the words of Francis Parkman, those of a mission and a trading station, and it was

[1] *Roman Provincial Administration*, pp. 5, 22.

not until the reign of Louis XIV that it became in the true sense a colony.[1] The object of Louis XIV and his advisers was to reproduce France in America, to make Canada in fact, as in name, New France. With this object the forms and customs of the old world were transplanted into the new, and a feudal system was created on American soil, and came into being not as a historic growth, but by order of a despotic king. 'An ignorant population, sprung from a brave and active race, but trained to sub-jection and dependence through centuries of feudal and monarchical despotism, was planted in the wilderness by the hand of authority, and told to grow and flourish. Artificial stimulants were applied, but freedom was withheld.'[1] Parkman goes on to tell us that 'the Canadian Government was essentially military',[1] and that the population in large measure sprang from soldiers and was recruited by disbanded soldiers. For instance, some companies of the famous Carignan-Salières regiment, which had been sent on service to Canada, were disbanded in Canada, the officers were converted into seigniors, and the non-commissioned officers and men held grants of land from their former officers. The Royal 'Inten-dant' of Canada, Talon, who proposed and carried out this scheme, in recommending it to Louis XIV and his minister, Colbert, gave Roman military colonization as a precedent,[2] and it has been pointed

---

[1] *The Old Régime in Canada*, 1885 ed., pp. 107, 394, 398.
[2] See Munro's *Seigniorial System in Canada*, p. 68 and note.

out in a previous chapter that French settlement in Canada had much in common with Roman colonization. Canada then, or rather the Province of Quebec, was settled by the French on a purely artificial system, the only natural element in it being that the colonists were given the same conditions—artificial conditions—that they had known in the Motherland. Lord Durham's verdict upon the French Canadians in his report was that ' They remain an old and stationary society, in a new and progressive world ',[1] and he recommended the fusion of Upper and Lower Canada in order to absorb this old-world conservatism of French Canada. The seigniorial system was eventually abolished, but French Canada still bears witness to the strength and permanence of a colonization carried out on purely artificial lines. As part of the British Empire, French Canada has been, in spite of Lord Durham's recommendation, allowed in the main to take its own line of development, and the result is that French Canadians to-day are more nearly allied to the French of the eighteenth century than to the French of modern France. In other words, a colony which owed its inception to the will of a king and was organized under hard and fast rules made by a king, which was artificial in every sense, except that the artificiality was reproduced from the old home, has held with singular tenacity to its original character.

Now, if we turn to the boundaries of Canada, we

[1] *Lord Durham's Report*, 1912 ed., vol. ii, p. 31.

can hardly find any other country in the world whose limits are so obviously artificial. There is nothing whatever natural about the international boundary between Canada and the United States. For a long distance, it simply follows a parallel of latitude. At some points, as in the north-east, where the Maine boundary question in past years nearly brought on war between Great Britain and the United States, or in the region of the Lake of the Woods, the boundary is almost grotesquely contrary to nature. The whole line is the result of treaties made before the geography was known, of subsequent interpretations of the treaties, and of political compromises. The gradual delimitation of this unnatural and inconvenient boundary left Canada, or rather British North America, the very antipodes of a compact territory. It was in short little more than a geographical expression. What was the agency which gave it cohesion and the beginning of a national existence? The answer is railways, the Intercolonial railway which was the condition of the Maritime Provinces federating with the Canadas, and the Canadian Pacific railway which was the condition of British Columbia entering the Dominion of Canada. No single work of man in any part of the world at any period of the world's history has so obviously and directly contributed to the making of a nation as the transcontinental railway in Canada. That Canada to-day is a Dominion from sea to sea is not the result of nature, it is the result of human handiwork, though behind that handiwork, it is true to say that there was the instinct of nationality.

This instinct, if not called into being, was and is most powerfully nourished by the neighbourhood of the United States, of an always present, in the past not always friendly, power, not separated by any natural boundary and possessing all the attractiveness of strength, wealth, kindred race, and language. It was in order to resist this attraction that Lord Durham recommended the union of British North America, so that the danger of being absorbed into the United States might be met 'by raising up for the North American colonist some nationality of his own'.[1]   Canadian statesmen feared that Canada might be absorbed not only by conquest but, in the alternative, by peaceful means and financial pressure. This was in large measure the origin of the policy of high protective tariffs, which was advocated and carried by Sir John Macdonald as a national policy, and which has held its ground to the present day as being a national policy.   In other words, once more the artificial has, with a view to preserving national existence in Canada, been set against the natural. From first to last Canada is an instance of a nation growing up not on the lines of nature but rather in transgression of those lines.   The original colonists were planted out by rule, they have never amalgamated with the race which came in after them so

[1] 1912 ed., vol. ii, p. 311.

that there should be race cohesion through the whole Dominion, that Dominion has the most unnatural boundary, the cohesion which it has attained is the direct result of scientific invention, and nationhood has been safeguarded by the most artificial of all human devices, a Protective Tariff. Yet Canada, thus constituted, bids fair to lead the British Empire and has already achieved a high place among the peoples of the world.

In order to avoid as far as possible matters of current controversy, it is not proposed to enter upon any detailed discussion in this book of the merits and demerits of preferential tariffs. It may well or plausibly be argued that the great natural resources of new countries are the secret of their history, that where land is abundant, population small, and means of living plentiful, political experiments are not so dangerous and harmful as in matured communities, and that, therefore, the root of the matter is after all in the natural and not in the artificial. Free Trade represented in England the triumph of the school according to nature, and Free Trade went hand in hand with Self-Government for the Colonies. Both the one and the other were considered to be according to nature, and it was held that nature should not be hampered by man. It is, therefore, worth noting that the father of Free Trade, Adam Smith, has a good word for the Navigation Acts, which especially embodied the old mercantile system. 'As defence', he writes, 'is of much more importance than opulence, the act of navigation is, perhaps, the wisest of all the commercial regulations of England.'[1]   It may be pointed out again that if, as has been contended in a previous chapter, the family analogy gives a true representation of the relations that exist or ought to exist between Great Britain and the Self-Governing Dominions, Imperial Preference, the root principle of which is membership of the same family, is in its essence far more natural than Free Trade which draws no distinction between members of the family and aliens.   Further, it is most noteworthy that the young nations of the Empire, having been given self-government, in other words, having been set free from artificial restrictions imposed by the Mother Country and left to develop on natural lines, have, from the instinct of self-preservation or other causes, shown a strong preference for the artificial as opposed to the natural.

The case of Canada has been quoted.   Let us take Australia.   The doctrine of the school according to nature is that goods and men should as far as possible come and go at will without artificial restrictions.   Australia is an island continent colonized from Great Britain, and Great Britain very wisely obeyed the call of nature and threw the reins on the necks of Australians, giving them their heads in the race for destiny.   The result has been that they have turned in the making of their nation to the artificial, to high tariffs and to race exclusion.   There

[1] *Wealth of Nations*, Bk. IV, chap. ii.

are very good reasons in either case ; and Australians are the rightful keepers of the future of Australia and the best judges of Australian interests. But here we have a curious contrast between the Roman and the British Empires. The Roman Empire was a triumph of the artificial, a military despotism. Yet in this artificial whole, and to some extent because it was artificial, that is to say because force prevailed and meant comparative peace, natural conditions prevailed to a considerable extent in this locality and in that. There was an absence of political freedom, but there was no want of living according to nature. Especially it should be noted that under this artificial régime, and because it was artificial, because it was made to order, and the will of the Central Government was imposed on the parts, there was, in spite of considerable variety of taxation, to which further reference will be made, probably more Free Trade and fewer Customs barriers in the Roman Empire than in the British Empire, which is the out-come of Self-Government and Free Trade combined.

The British Empire has, it must be repeated, had in its composition much more of the natural and much less of the artificial than was the case with the Roman Empire ; and in the counsels of British statesmen in the nineteenth century the natural pre-vailed to an extent to which it would be difficult to find a parallel. But in this Empire, and in those parts of it where the intention was most clearly shown that development should be on natural lines, there the world has learnt the lesson that artificial restrictions commend themselves to the instincts of young peoples, who do not feel safe in entrusting their future to the course of nature. They may be wrong; they may be short-sighted and erring unwittingly against the light; but the fact remains that, while England through obedience to natural laws has given that freedom which has enabled the Empire to be a nursery of young peoples, the young peoples judge that they can only fulfil their destinies as nations by calling in the artificial, not merely to supplement, but in large measure to counteract nature.

Closely akin to the antithesis of the natural and the artificial is that of facts and appearances. Do not tell me what this man or this thing looks like, the whole question is what he or it is. That is a very common form of expression, which commends itself as being downright, going to the root of the matter, and indicating the view of an honest, straight-thinking man. It is a most dangerous view, if applied wholesale to Empires.

In his Essay on the Government of Dependencies, at the conclusion of the chapter on the ' Advantages derived by the Dominant Country from its Supremacy over a Dependency', Sir George Cornewall Lewis discusses the ' supposed advantages flowing from the possession of dependencies, which are expressed in terms so general and vague, that they cannot be referred to any determinate head. Such, for example, is the glory which a country is supposed to derive from an extensive colonial Empire.' He dismisses the subject by saying 'that a nation derives no true glory from any possession which produces no assignable advantage to itself or to other communities', that, if a country receives no access of strength, no commercial advantages and so forth from a dependency, to be set against the evils of dependence, 'such a possession cannot justly be called glorious.'[1] The writer, though he published his book in 1841, after *Lord Durham's Report* had seen the light, conceived of a colonial Empire as consisting solely of dependencies. He had no vision of a system containing alike dependencies and Self-Governing Dominions, and he uses the word glory to emphasize his argument that appearance without fact behind it is nothing worth. Even glory is something more than vainglory. A nation does not win glory without thereby deriving some permanent result, good or bad, upon the character and the thought of its members. But if for the word glory we substitute prestige or credit, we realize that appearances may be in themselves substantial facts. The word prestige has been attacked—much as Cornewall Lewis attacked glory—as being a foreign word importing an idea of bombast, which is, or ought to be, foreign to Englishmen. Credit, on the contrary, is well known in matter of fact commercial circles. A merchant trades in great measure on credit. It is

---

[1] *Government of Dependencies*, 1891 ed., pp. 233-4.

possible that he may have little or no actual cash behind it, but if he possesses credit, in other words, if he is believed to be a man of substance, he can carry on transactions which would otherwise be out of his reach. Appearance in this case is an actual fact. Similarly, nations also largely live on credit, they are largely judged by appearances, even more so than individuals, because they are less liable to daily close inspection from experts.

Further, the more competition there is, the more important appearances are. The Roman Empire for the greater part of its existence had no competition, it was in the position of a successful monopolist, and the Romans were so assured in their position that appearances mattered less to them than to us. Yet it can hardly be doubted that their Empire would not have held out so long, in its time of decay, had it not been for credit and appearance exceeding the actual facts of the case. The shadow of the Roman Empire was something without the substance. The Empire looked stronger than it really was in its later days, and the Roman name alone was an asset. Our Empire is far from holding the unchallenged position which the Romans so long enjoyed, and appearances are proportionately more important to us. Let us suppose that, as a matter of fact, we derived from the Dominions and dependencies beyond the seas no advantage whatever in commerce, or for defence purposes, or in any other direction. Still the fact would remain that the British Empire looks large on the map; that the world in general, the man in the street, judges of men and things by what they look like, not by what they are; that our Empire on the map, on the one hand, suggests much to be taken by those who are prepared to go to war, and, on the other hand, gives an appearance of strength which would be wholly wanting, if Great Britain had no oversea possessions. In short, those who try to estimate aright the value of our Empire will never leave out of sight the importance of appearances, which are even more potent in days like our own of widely spread half knowledge, than in former times of fairly general ignorance.

There is yet another side to this subject of appearances. In *Ancient and Modern Imperialism* Lord Cromer, like Mr. Arnold who has been quoted above, places the Romans far ahead of any modern nation in power of assimilating subject races. They had, he thinks, a much easier task than has fallen to the lot of modern Empires, for they were not confronted by the difficulties of colour and religion which are obstacles to us. At any rate, they were more successful in Romanizing other races than the nations of modern Europe have been in assimilating their subjects. Among these modern nations the English are generally supposed to have less capacity for assimilation than, at any rate, the Latin peoples. Lord Cromer holds that ' our habits are insular, and our social customs render us, in comparison at all events with the Latin races, somewhat unduly exclusive'. On the other hand, he gives as the result of his almost unrivalled experience, 'the conclusion that the British generally, though they succeed less well when once the full tide of education has set in, possess in a very high degree the power of acquiring the sympathy and confidence of any primitive races with which they are brought in contact.'[1] Similarly, Mr. Arnold writes of the Romans: 'Rome was extraordinarily successful in civilizing barbarians, not perhaps so successful in dealing with races already of a high type.'[2] In comparing the English with other modern Europeans in this matter of assimilation, Lord Cromer finds that while the English are wanting in 'social adaptability, in which the French excel', they have, on the other hand, 'a relatively high degree of administrative and political elasticity.'[3] These views may be summed up as follows. The Romans were more successful in assimilation than any modern nation, partly because in the Western provinces a larger proportion of their subjects were in a primitive stage and, therefore, ready for the melting pot than has been the case in modern Empires. The higher and more civilized races are, the more difficult they are to assimilate, because they are more stereotyped; and, lastly, assimilation has two sides, what Lord Cromer calls

[1] *Ancient and Modern Imperialism*, pp. 74–5.
[2] *Roman Provincial Administration*, p. 6.
[3] *Ancient and Modern Imperialism*, pp. 84–5.

'social adaptability', and what he calls 'administrative and political elasticity'.

Now if the English, by common consent, have been wanting in 'social adaptability', it is because they are more indifferent than other peoples to appearances. If, by common consent, they have been successful as administrators and makers of Empire, it is precisely for the same reason, that they have disregarded appearances, cared little for logic and uniformity and dealt with facts. But in proportion to the success brought by administrative and political elasticity is the drawback arising from absence of social adaptability; for the better the work done by the makers, and the more they have raised the peoples under them, and given them cohesion and civilization, the more these peoples, having secured the substance, look for and appreciate appearances. Consequently, the further the constructive work of the Empire is carried, the more attention appearances ought to receive. Nor does the question of appearances concern only the relations of the British to coloured races. It concerns the relations between the different groups of our own race. The British from beyond the seas too often find the British in the home land reserved and uncongenial. The home Briton can hardly be considered successful in assimilating the overseas Briton. The reason usually given is that the home Briton is stiff and formal, in other words, what is generally classed under the term artificial. But the truer explanation is that the home Briton is too natural, he does not care for appearances or estimate them at their proper value.   If he could really become more artificial, he would seem more natural.   In short, if we desire to keep goodwill among the nations of our Empire, we must pay more regard to appearances.

CHAPTER IX

THE TWO EMPIRES

How far was the Roman Empire, and how far is the British Empire, one Empire?

It is not easy to gather the answer to the question as regards the Roman Empire from those who have written with authority on the subject. Cornewall Lewis says, ' The regulations respecting the appointment, powers, and rank of the Roman governors, and the duration of their office, constituted the only part of the provincial institutions of Rome which were uniform throughout the Provinces. In all other respects there was the utmost diversity in the provincial governments. It was the general policy of the Romans not to make more changes in a conquered territory than were necessary for reducing it to complete subjection.' [1] Mr. Arnold writes, ' It is exceedingly difficult in discussing the Provinces of Rome not to talk of them as a whole, and as a fixed whole. But, in truth, the Roman world is a world continually growing, developing, changing, always tending to a uniformity but never fully reaching it. The difference between East and West is never obliterated, and at last victoriously asserts itself.

[1] *Government of Dependencies*, pp. 119–20.

K 2

The Romans showed greater power of assimilation than has been shown by any other conquerors ; but even they could not assimilate a civilization like that of Greece, which was in some respects superior to their own. So the Greek East was not organized, after the strict type of the Roman Province, into colonies and *municipia* until a late date.' But he goes on to note, ' the large and increasing element of unity. The administration was everywhere of much the same type.'[1] Professor Bury tells us that ' The Roman world was a complex of different nations and languages, without a really deep-reaching unity, held together so long by the mere brute strength of tyrannical Roman universality, expressed in one law, one official language, and one Emperor —a merely external union. Naturally it fell into two worlds, the Greek (once the Dominion of Alexander) and the Roman ; and this natural division finally asserted itself and broke the artificial globe of the Roman Universe.' This passage emphasizes the artificial character of the Roman Empire, a point which has been discussed in the last chapter ; and it seems at first to suggest, as Mr. Arnold's words also suggest, that the Roman Empire was two Empires in one ; but Professor Bury goes on to negative any such conclusion. ' The actual territorial division between the sons of Theodosius did not theoretically constitute two Roman Empires ' ; and in the Preface to his volume, he is at pains to con-

[1] *Roman Provincial Administration*, pp. 5–7.

tradict the commonly received doctrine that the
Empire broke up into an Eastern and a Western
Empire. ' Nothing can be easier than to apprehend
that the Roman Empire endured, one and undivided, however changed and dismembered, from
the first century B.C. to the fifteenth century A.D.' [1]
His view is borne out by Professor Freeman's words
quoted in the last chapter.[2]

The Roman Empire was necessarily very different
in one era from what it was in another. After
Diocletian, for instance, had handled and recast it,
it was widely different from the Empire which
Augustus left behind him. It may, therefore, well
be objected to any comparison between the Roman
Empire and the British Empire at the present day,
that the Roman Empire was one thing in one
century and another thing in another, just as the
British Empire at the end of the nineteenth century
was poles asunder from the British Empire at the
end of the eighteenth century, and still more at the
end of the seventeenth century, so far as it then
existed. But the objection is not wholly a valid
one. The true conclusion seems to be that, in spite
of the manifold changes which time wrought, in
spite of the statesmanlike disregard for uniformity
which the Romans showed in their best days, in
spite of their toleration of local creeds and usages,

[1] *A History of the Later Roman Empire*, vol. i, p. 36, and Preface,
p. viii.
[2] Above, p. 115.

the Roman Empire, so far as it was an Empire, that
is so far as it was a political organization, was from
first to last one Empire. If it was artificial, ' a
merely external union,' at any rate it was all
artificial. It was one, whichever way we look at it.

It was one in authority, even when emperors
were multiplied. The *imperium*, we have seen,
was one and undivided. At head-quarters, at any
rate in the early days of the Empire, the Emperor
had all the powers of the State in his own hands.
He had no departmental ministers, recognized as
such, no Foreign Secretary, no Secretary of State for
the Colonies.[1] The nearest approach to any division
of authority was the allotment of the Provinces
made by Augustus between the Emperor and the
Senate, but the real power remained with the
Emperor. In each Province again, when the Empire
was at its best and strongest, the governor was
supreme in all respects and combined all powers.
' The special feature of the Roman system was its
union in one single head and hand of functions
which the modern system takes care to separate.'[2]
It is true that the time was when in the British
Empire also the governor of a colony was actually,
as he still is nominally, commander-in-chief, when

---

[1] Mr. Arnold in *Roman Provincial Administration*, p. 133, in writing
of the early Roman Empire, says, ' The Emperor was assisted by his
Cabinet ; and his secretaries for the conduct of the different branches
of the administration became ministers of state,' but no authority is
quoted for this statement.

[2] Arnold l. c. p. 54

he had judicial functions, inasmuch as his Executive Council was a Court of Appeal, while he always was, and in the Crown Colonies still is, directly responsible for the finances. It is also true that, in the later days of the Roman Empire, the command of the troops in those Provinces in which legions were stationed, was separated from the charge of the Civil Administration ; so that it might be argued that the position and powers of a governor of a Roman Province did not widely differ from those of a governor of a British Crown Colony, if they are compared at corresponding epochs of history. But it was not so. The perfection of the Roman system was union of all authority in one person. The perfection of the British system is entrusting different functions to different hands. In its essence the Roman system was an undivided despotism. Mr. Arnold sums it up in the words, ' Rome had undertaken an impossible task, that of ruling an immense Empire without federation and without a representative system, where the sole sources of power were the Supreme Central Government and the army.' [1] It seems strange to say that the task was impossible, when it was performed so long and so efficiently, and it has yet to be proved in the history of the world that a military despotism in Roman hands was not as long-lived as, or more long-lived than, sounder systems in other hands. But there will always be two opposite points of view

[1] *Roman Provincial Administration*, p. 168.

from which the Roman Empire can be regarded,
one which seeks for the reasons why it declined
and fell ; the other—surely the wiser one—which
tries to discover why this Empire lasted so long.
From either point of view, however, it can be
summed up that in the matter of authority the
Roman Empire was one, the result of a single
military despotism.

It was one in kind, too. Great as the Empire
was, it hardly reached, in its southernmost limits,
in Egypt and Arabia, to the Tropic of Cancer. The
North of England or the South of Scotland was its
northernmost bound. It took in East and West,
but only the Nearer East, and the West only in
Europe and North Africa. It was in the main
a Mediterranean Empire, all or nearly all within the
temperate zone, not concerned with lands of great
cold, not concerned with the Tropics, not concerned,
as has been said, to any appreciable extent, with
coloured races. The Provinces differed one from
another in this respect or in that. The Greek East,
as a whole, differed from the Roman West. But all
the Provinces in East and West alike were of the
same general type. All bore the hall-mark of town
life. All were thoroughly conquered ; all were
partially colonized ; ' and, as the franchise becomes
more and more extended, the Roman law comes to
be the only law over the whole Empire.' [1]

---

[1] Arnold's *Roman Provincial Administration*, p. 32.

It was one again in revenue matters. The receipts from the taxes, other than octrois and municipal taxes, all went to the Imperial Treasury, as we should now call it, including (as long as the provinces were divided between the Senate and the Emperor) both the aerarium and the fiscus. It is true that, not being ' cursed with the passion for uniformity ', and very probably acting on their favourite principle of *divide et impera*, the Romans allowed considerable varieties of taxation as between the different provinces. Even the Portoria, or customs duties, were not uniform. ' In this respect the Empire never formed a united whole, but was divided into a number of large customs districts, within which the scale of the tax varied considerably.' [1] The customs duties were as a rule *ad valorem* duties, but the rate varied. Five per cent. was charged in Sicily on imports or exports, $2\frac{1}{2}$ per cent. in Gaul or Asia. The duties were levied for revenue, not for protective purposes, but we have an indication of protective duties as against the foreigner, in that ' the Egyptian ports were, if not directly barred, at any rate practically closed, by differential custom dues against Arabian and Indian transports '.[2] No doubt taxation within the Roman Empire was far from uniform, but for diversity of tariffs the Roman provinces would not compare with

---

[1] *The Imperial Civil Service of Rome*, by H. Mattingly (Cambridge Historical Essays, No. xviii), 1910, p. 10.
[2] Mommsen's *Provinces of the Roman Empire*, vol. ii, p. 299.

the British Crown Colonies, let alone the self-governing Dominions. The reason is that the tariffs in the different British colonies or dependencies are, with some few exceptions, as when British Free Trade may have dictated to India, arranged in the interests of each colony or dependency. The Romans, on the contrary, from beginning to end, never let go the principle of tribute to the central power. The provinces were to pay the cost of their Government, but the surplus was to go to Rome. Financially, as in other respects, the Empire was one.

Bacon's view of the Roman Empire is specially interesting, because he lived just at the time when England was on the threshold of her Empire work. Roman colonization, it has been seen, was mainly military colonization, but what Bacon found to admire in the Romans was the extent to which they went beyond the mere planting of garrisons in conquered countries. 'I find,' he wrote, or rather pleaded, 'by the best opinions, that there be two means to assure and retain in obedience countries conquered, both very differing, almost in extremes, the one towards the other. The one is by colonies and intermixture of people, and transplantation of families ... and it was indeed the Roman manner; but this is like an old relic, much reverenced and almost never used. But the other, which is the modern manner, and almost wholly in practice and use, is by garrisons and citadels, and lists or companies of men of war, and other like matters of terror and bridle.'[1] The Roman Empire, in his view, was the result of conquest, but of conquest assured by colonization and widening of citizenship, whereby, to quote again words of his which have already been quoted, 'It was not the Romans that spread upon the world, but it was the world that spread upon the Romans.'[2] Up to Bacon's time Empire had been synonymous with conquest, and the Spanish conquest of America, which was before his eyes and within his ken, must have seemed another illustration of overrunning a world. To him the Romans stood out as being more than mere conquerors. Where they conquered, they colonized also. 'Ubicunque vicit Romanus habitat.'[3] But Bacon's words bear witness to the fact that this great Roman Empire was one, and one only. All of it was the result of conquest; in all of it there was something more than conquest. No part of the Empire contrasted with another part, as being different in kind, it was all one Empire.

What would Bacon have said of the present British Empire? He could only have come to the conclusion that it is two Empires in one, that this fact marks it out from all the Empires of the world. Before enlarging upon this feature of duality in the British Empire as contrasted with the unity of the

---

[1] 'Case of the Post Nati of Scotland,' Spedding's edition, vol. vii, p. 661.

[2] 'Of the True Greatness of Kingdoms and Estates,' Spedding's edition, vol. vi, p. 448.

[3] Seneca, *Dialogues*, xii. 7. 7.

Roman Empire, there are two points to be noticed
which are at least interesting for the purposes of
comparing ancient and modern history. We are
taking what was incomparably the greatest Empire
of the ancient world side by side with the greatest
Empire up to date of modern times, and we have seen
that the greatest ancient Empire was one in authority
and in kind, all in the same zone, in the main
continuous, compact, and practically coterminous
with civilization. Now the most remote province
of this great ancient Empire was part, not all (for
the Roman province of Britain at no time included
either Ireland or the Highlands of Scotland), of the
motherland and centre of the great modern Empire ;
and this modern Empire lies almost entirely outside
the limits of the ancient Empire. Gibraltar, Malta,
and Cyprus were within Roman bounds, and Egypt,
though not part of the British Empire, may be said
to be under British hegemony or protection not very
far removed from its status in regard to Rome under
the later Ptolemies, before it definitely became a
Roman province ; but otherwise the whole of the
British Empire is in parts of the world which Rome
never knew and which never knew Rome. Moreover, we have the interesting fact that, while the
Roman Empire was all in one zone, which contributed to its unity, that zone and the Roman part
of it has become, beyond all other regions of the
world, split up into separate and independent nations.
On the other hand, where England has overflowed

into temperate zones like her own, she has found them wholly outside Europe, and very largely in the most remote part of the world, in the far south. The contrast between the Roman and British Empires is illustrated and emphasized, if it is borne in mind that they are in the main geographically exclusive of each other ; and yet we have this curious half-link between them, historical and geographical, that the most distant province of the Roman Empire, cut off by the sea from the main body, became the heart and nucleus of the modern Empire.

The second point concerns the diversity of the British Empire as compared with the unity of the Roman Empire. What was it that made the Roman Empire one ? The answer, which has already been given, is loss or absence of freedom. It became more one in proportion as liberty disappeared. In the same proportion the British Empire has become less one as freedom has grown. The Roman system produced a structure which lasted for almost if not quite an unparalleled time, but we are told to believe that it lasted, as an old oak lasts, more dead than alive, and perished because the source of life, which is freedom, was dried up. It is for the future to show—and herein lies the intense interest of the British Empire—whether the diversity in that Empire, being born of freedom, will preserve the life of the whole, whether the true road to unity is through diversity, because diversity means freedom.

The British Empire, it has been suggested, is two Empires in one. It falls into two wholly different, and in the main, mutually exclusive spheres, which may be distinguished as the sphere of rule and the sphere of settlement. It is obvious that these two spheres differ wholly in kind. The sphere of rule is an Empire over tropical lands and coloured races. There the English have come, not to settle, but to administer and to rule wholly alien peoples. The sphere of settlement is an Empire of dwelling-places in lands which are outside the tropics and inside the temperate zones. It is an Empire not over but in the hands of white races, mainly our own British race. The English have come there to settle in the lands, to make them British, to rule the lands, it is true, but mainly to rule themselves. Reproduction is the key-note of the sphere of settlement, governance is the key-note of the sphere of rule. Of the sphere of rule it may be said that the English are in it but not of it; of the sphere of settlement that the English are both in it and of it; and this difference is illustrated by the fact that the self-governing Dominions are all British soil, all lands held in complete sovereignty and ownership, whereas a considerable proportion of the sphere of rule is technically only under British Protectorate.

In kind, then, there are two British Empires, not one. How does it stand in the matter of authority? The whole of the British possessions are the King's dominions, whether they are in the sphere of rule or in the sphere of settlement. It cannot be too strongly emphasized that allegiance to one King, to one Crown, is the greatest of all bonds of union in the British Empire. Nor can it be overlooked that the bond is not merely to the Crown as representing the State or the race, but is also a personal tie to the King for the time reigning, all the stronger when, as in the case of his present Majesty, the reigning King has in a unique degree personal knowledge of all parts of his dominions. This loyalty to a person is liable to be underrated. One of the great mistakes made by the English after the conquest of Canada was to overlook the fact that French-Canadian loyalty had been to persons rather than to institutions; and at the time wise governors, like Carleton, emphasized, though with little or no result, the importance of making the Canadians feel that under British rule they were still the King's men. Especially is this personal side of the monarchy to be borne in mind in regard to Eastern races, and herein lay the statesmanship of creating the title Emperor of India. But taking the Crown as the embodiment of authority, how far is it one? It has been said that though Roman Emperors were multiplied, the authority was one. There is but one Crown in the British Empire. Does it represent undivided authority? His Majesty the King is Emperor of India, he is the constitutional King of Canada; he is the Ruler of India in a wholly different sense from that in which he is King of Canada. This means one person representing two kinds of authority, as opposed to the later stages of the Roman Empire when there were more Emperors than one but only one authority. But this statement does not quite meet the case. There is division of authority, but the root of the division is not, so to speak, in the Crown itself, it is in the advisers of the Crown. Great Britain has acquired an Empire; part of that Empire Great Britain rules, the other part is not ruled by Great Britain, but is a reproduction or reproductions of Great Britain. His Majesty is the constitutional King of Great Britain. Therefore, both as regards the United Kingdom itself and as regards the parts of his dominions which are ruled by the United Kingdom, he is, whether as Emperor or as King, advised by the Ministry of Great Britain. His Majesty is the constitutional King of each of the reproductions of Great Britain, that is to say, of each of the self-governing Dominions, but here, through his representative in each Dominion, he is primarily advised, not by the Ministry of Great Britain, but by the Ministry of the Dominion. In this lies the division of authority, which did not exist in the Roman Empire, even when the Roman Empire had no longer a single head.

The general statement has been made that the British Empire is two Empires in one, each Empire outside the other. It is a statement which is broadly true, sufficiently true to give a fairly accurate bird's-eye view of the whole. But, as a matter of fact, in the first place, the two spheres of rule and settlement are not quite mutually exclusive ; and, in the second place, each of the two spheres contains so many diverse elements, that it may be argued that the British Empire is not merely two Empires in one but many Empires in one. A few words will illustrate each of these two points. The sphere of settlement is not purely a sphere of settlement. In other words, the Self-Governing Dominions are not exclusively inhabited by incomers of the white races. All of them had once aboriginal inhabitants. The aboriginal natives are now extinct in Newfoundland and Tasmania. In Canada, and still more on the continent of Australia, they are—from any other than a philanthropic point of view—a negligeable quantity ; but in New Zealand the Maoris are a very appreciable element in the population, and in South Africa the coloured men largely outnumber the white, making the native question the greatest of all South African problems. Nor are the Self-Governing Dominions all outside the tropics. The South African Union touches the tropic of Capricorn in the north of the Transvaal. The whole of the north of Australia is within the tropics ; and Australia has a tropical dependency in Papua, as has New Zealand in the Cook Islands. If, on the other hand, we turn to what has been styled the sphere of rule, we find that, so far from all of it being included in the tropics or all of it the home of coloured races, the Mediterranean colonies are within this sphere, so are the Falkland Islands, so is Bermuda, which last colony is largely self-governing. If we go inside the tropics again, to the West Indies, here are tropical islands which have been the scene of British settlement since the seventeenth century, and which had a large measure of self-government long before any one of the present Self-Governing Dominions, except Newfoundland and the Province of Nova Scotia, had any connexion whatever with the British Empire.

Within each of the two spheres the diversities are great. In the sphere of settlement not only has South Africa a native problem, which Canada and Australia have not; not only are Canada and South Africa differentiated from Australia and New Zealand in that from the beginning of colonization Canada had the French element in its white population and South Africa the Dutch; but in this very respect in which they differ from Australasia, Canada and South Africa may be compared and contrasted in various ways. For instance, the French Canadians are much more concentrated in one part of the Dominion of Canada than is the case with the Dutch in South Africa, and again the only political liberty which the French Canadians have known in their history has been in the form of self-government on the British model and under the British flag, whereas some of the Dutch in South Africa have known political liberty in other forms. It is important to emphasize that the Self-Governing Dominions differ so greatly from one another, that they have diverse elements, white and coloured, in their populations, and conditions varying according to latitude and longitude and land and sea ; for one main cause of inaccurate thinking on the problem of the relations between the Dominions and the Mother Country is that that problem is usually presented as one between two parties only, the Dominions on the one side, and the Mother Country on the other, whereas we have not to go farther than the Imperial Conferences to find abundant illustration of the fact that the divergence between one Dominion and another is as great as or greater than the divergence between any one of the Dominions and the Mother Country.

Has Australia, for instance, more in common with South Africa or with the United Kingdom? In common with South Africa and as against the United Kingdom, it has space and youth. It has its bush as South Africa has its veldt, it has not a few similarities to South Africa in climate, products, water supply or want of water, and so forth. Both are young communities in a somewhat similar stage of development ; they will to some extent compare in numbers of the population. On the other hand, Australia has practically no native problem, and in race and all that race brings with it is as British as England herself. How can the problem of Empire be rightly presented as one between Great Britain and Australia, or one between Great Britain and South Africa, and never as between Australia and South Africa, and so forth of the other Dominions?

To speak and write and think of the Self-Governing Dominions in their relations to the Mother Country as a homogeneous whole leads to misapprehension of the difficulties and the possibilities of the British Empire, but it is still more misleading, though it is hardly so common a failing, to overlook the vast difference between the various dependencies which are included in the sphere of rule. What could be more different than Gibraltar from Fiji, the Malay Peninsula from the Falkland Islands, India from West Africa? It has been seen that some of the West Indian islands, Barbados for instance, with its long record of British colonization and representative institutions, have historically a claim to be placed in the sphere of settlement. India again is on a wholly different plane from West Africa, and is so completely organized as a unit, so equipped with a complete administration, that it has been a question whether it should not be one of the parties to Imperial Conferences. Further, there is this interesting and notable feature in India that as Great Britain has colonized the Dominions, so India, through the operation of the indentured coolie system, has colonized not a few of the other tropical dependencies of the Empire, Mauritius, Trinidad, British Guiana, Fiji. It has, in short, to some extent supplemented Great Britain in the British Empire by playing the part of a Mother Country.

But if we take the case of India, as being the British dependency which is on the highest plane,

we shall find that there is in real truth a great gulf
fixed between the sphere of rule and the sphere of
settlement, and that gulf to some extent coincides
with the difference between the Roman and the
British Empires.

The Self-Governing Dominions have become self-
governing, because self-government is inherent in
the British race; the grant of self-government to
these British communities has, therefore, been in the
course of nature. This note runs through Lord
Durham's report. He proposed to give self-government to the French Canadians only as part of and
merged in a British nationality. Even if the French
and Dutch were not, as they are, being white and
western nations, infinitely more akin to the English
in political views and traditions, than any coloured
people of the Empire, there is the fact that in Canada
the British element outnumbers the French, and in
South Africa is on an equality with the Dutch.
Therefore, in the present Self-Governing Dominions
it may be said that self-government is the result of
natural evolution. But India—to take the greatest
and in the work of construction perhaps the most
advanced of the British dependencies—never has
been and never will be made British by settlement.
If it were to be placed in the category of self-
governing peoples, it would be placed in a category
to which it does not naturally belong, and it would
be endowed with entirely alien institutions, which
for many generations to come would be hardly

intelligible, much less beneficial, to its millions of inhabitants.

Further, the above argument assumes what many authorities have warned us is not and never has been the case, that India is one, instead of being the home of the most diverse races, creeds, classes, and sorts and conditions of men. In Lord Durham's report self-government was to be the concomitant of union, and responsible government has attained or is attaining its fullest expression in groups of kindred communities, made or being made by union or federation into larger wholes. Such unity as there is in India has not sprung from the people or the soil. It is the result, as the Roman Empire was, of all the diverse elements being controlled by one alien rule, which has produced, again to quote Professor Bury's words applied to the Roman Empire, 'a merely external union.' If self-government were granted to India, this bond of union would largely disappear, and the diversities would prevail. It would be impossible to estimate how many generations must pass away before union, which must be the basis of self-government, can come from below not from above, from within not from without.

India, which perhaps of all parts of the British Empire is most nearly akin to a Roman Province, has been taken as the British dependency which is on the highest plane. It is on the highest plane, partly because there has been in this great Eastern land a civilization unknown to negro or Pacific lands of barbarism, partly because British constructive administration has here been longest at work, and has found its widest and fullest field. But the fact that India, or part of India, has been the home of a civilization of its own, does not necessarily make it a more promising area for future self-government. The conservatism of the East is proverbial, and lands which have known no government at all, other than barbaric usage, may conceivably be a more congenial soil for planting alien institutions than one which possesses a system or systems deep rooted in the past.

British constructive administration in India has been successful, not as having brought in political institutions of a British type, but as having bettered what was in India already, that is more or less personal rule. It has given what was and is understood, and not a House of Commons, which would not be understood. Self-government implies the many, not the few; and it is not until the many have in the long course of ages been wholly transformed that the sphere of rule can be assimilated to the sphere of settlement, though the few may be and are being increasingly associated in the work and training which rule implies.

It is then roughly true to say that the British Empire is two Empires in one. Let us suppose, by way of further illustration, that the Empire consisted only either of the sphere of settlement or of the sphere of rule. Could we in either case find analogies? If there were no India and no Crown Colonies and Protectorates, the British Empire would consist of the United Kingdom, Canada, Newfoundland, Australia, New Zealand, and South Africa, forming a group or federation of self-governing communities, linked together in partnership under one Crown, and having in the United Kingdom a predominant and to some extent managing partner, for the reason that the United Kingdom is the ancestral home of the common King, that it formerly ruled the other partners, that it is the Motherland, and is still, though in a constantly decreasing proportion, far ahead in strength, wealth, and population. There is no analogy to be found to this political association, either in the Roman Empire or in any other ancient or modern Empire. At first sight, to compare great things with small, there was something resembling it in Greek history, in the famous confederacy of Delos, which started as a League of Sea States of kindred blood and origin, with a predominant partner in Athens, the league being formed for common defence purposes, and the partners contributing, some in money and some in ships, while the executive control was left in the hands of Athens as the predominant partner. If we could forget how the Ionian confederacy began and how it ended; if again the question of Naval Defence was, even more than it is, the all-absorbing question of our Empire; and if the Self-Governing Dominions left the control of their ships wholly in the hands of the Admiralty, we should find some parallel between the two cases. But this Greek league began with members which were entirely independent States, and ended with members which were tributary subjects of Athens. Our system is composed of units which have been steadily growing from subordination to equality and partnership. We cannot find analogies to the British Empire in Greece, because all the Greek colonies started as independent States. The Roman Empire gives us no parallel to our sphere of settlement, because its history is a history of taking away, not enlarging freedom. Nor does modern history give us anything with which to compare Great Britain and her colonies as opposed to her dependencies. We must comfort ourselves with having, for better or worse, presented the world with something wholly new.

If, on the other hand, we eliminate the Self-Governing Dominions, if the British Empire at the present day consisted solely of India and the Crown Colonies and Protectorates, we should have the case of a comparatively small but strong nation ruling absolutely territories and peoples in size and numbers out of all proportion to itself. The population of the United Kingdom at present far exceeds the combined populations of the Self-Governing Dominions, but it is small as compared with the population of India alone, leaving out of sight the Crown Colonies and Protectorates. Now so far as the keynote to this

side of the Empire is rule, we are coming somewhere
near to the Roman Empire, and there is this
interesting point to notice. The world grew upon
the Romans, says Bacon. It did so, in one sense
among others, that the acquisition of Provinces
called out the strong qualities of the Romans and
made them stronger. They became rulers because
they had to rule ; the Provinces were their training
ground, and the Western Provinces bred new rulers
for the Empire. Similarly every part of the world,
where British dependencies have been acquired, has
been a training ground for British administrators,
and traditions of rule have grown up and been handed
on. We have good reason for thinking that England
has done much for India, but she has also gained
much in possessing in India an unequalled school
wherein to learn the lessons of responsibility and
administration. The Romans and the British alike
had an innate capacity for ruling, which grew by
use ; but we have seen that the field in which this
quality was applied and trained was very different
in the two cases. In modern times, perhaps, the
nearest analogy to Great Britain and her sphere of
rule would be the Dutch and their colonial Empire,
both Great Britain and the British dependencies
being on a larger scale than the Netherlands and
the Dutch dependencies. It would be the nearest
analogy—though far from near—because in either
case trade has been the ultimate cause of the
acquisition of dependencies. With the Romans,

conquest brought trade in its train, and where the Romans conquered and where they traded, there they formed colonies and they ruled. With the English, trade begat acquisition of territory, and where the English traded and where they acquired territory, there they ruled. But in the sphere of rule, they did not form colonies, for British settlement in the West Indies is an exceptional case. Nothing could be more remote from the military colonization of the Roman Empire.

The question asked at the beginning of this chapter was, 'How far was the Roman Empire, and how far is the British Empire, one Empire?' The answer is that the Roman Empire was one, that the British Empire is two in one; that each of the two halves of the British Empire contains the most diverse elements; that one half is a political structure which has no common ground whatever with the Roman Empire and cannot be compared with it in any way; that the other half admits of comparison but still more of contrast.

CHAPTER X

THE BRITISH INSTINCT AND THE LAW OF NATIONAL LIFE

How did the Romans hold their Empire for so long a time? How has the British Empire been held together up to date? And by what means, judging from past experience, and from the signs of the times, are we likely to continue to hold it?

The answer to the first question has been abundantly given already. The Roman Empire was held by force, supplemented by assimilation, the nucleus of which assimilation was in the Roman colonies. It may be emphasized once more that the Romans used force so effectively and so continuously that they placed their Empire beyond the possibility of competition. It became not the strongest or greatest in a group of competing kingdoms, nations, or Empires, but for centuries practically the only Empire. According to the view which each student may take, it may be said to have lasted so long because it had killed out competitors, or to have decayed for want of competition. At any rate, the only civilized power which the barbarians living in the outer darkness had ever known or heard of was the Roman power.

There was no other power with which they could compare it.

In British history overseas much has turned and still turns, in many and different respects, on knowledge or want of knowledge, on ability or inability to compare. This can be illustrated on various sides, all of them interesting though not all germane to the subject of this chapter. In North America the relations between the colonies which now form the United States and the Mother Country suffered greatly because, communication being in the seventeenth and eighteenth centuries relatively worse than it was in the Roman Empire, the colonists did not at any given time know what Great Britain was doing at the other side of the world. They saw British mistakes under their eyes, but Marlborough's victories which, as a matter of fact, brought the Treaty of Utrecht and assured British possession of Nova Scotia, Newfoundland, and the coasts of Hudson Bay, being remote from them, were not compared with and weighed against failures in America. When the American War of Independence came on, the French Canadians, a lately conquered people and strongly attached to France, did not, with very few exceptions, rise against England, though invited to do so by the revolting colonies, largely because they had had opportunities of comparing the English from home with their English neighbours and former enemies in America. They did not want the English in any form, but of the two types they preferred the English from England. At the present day the negroes in the West Indies compare favourably their own status under England with the status of the negroes in the United States; and this comparison means a strong attachment to England in the black population of the West Indies. Take again the case of India. The natives of India only know British rule. They would probably appreciate it more fully, had they been able to compare it with other alien white rule. Where British rule is side by side with other European rule as in West Africa, there are clear indications that the native races prefer British rule. England, in her relations with native races, has gained greatly, not from the fact that the English are popular as a race, but from the fact that wherever there is a possibility of comparison, at any given time or place, some other people is usually found to be more unpopular. This feature did not enter into the Roman Empire, because it had no competitor, and because its basis openly and avowedly was force.

If the Roman Empire was held by force, how has the British Empire been held together up to date? Again, let us take separately the two separate halves of the Empire—the sphere of settlement and the sphere of rule.

The Self-Governing Dominions and the Mother Country have so far been held together, by starting, in the main, from a common origin, by allegiance to a common Crown, by the sentiment which a common origin and a common allegiance has created and preserved, by substantial advantages accruing to the Dominions from their connexion with the Mother Country, mainly protection from foreign enemies, and the supply of capital for purposes of development; and over and above these bonds of union, by the constant removal of restrictions on liberty and the steady encouragement of larger units. The policy which has produced existing conditions in the self-governing half of the British Empire originated in Lord Durham's report, and the essence of that report was that self-government is in British or Anglicized communities the basis of content, though the self-government which he sketched out for Canada fell very far short of self-government as we know it at the present day; that self-government should be preceded or accompanied by union of coterminous Provinces into one larger whole; and that this double process of giving freedom, and grouping into larger units, not only would be, but should avowedly be, in the interests of the Mother Country as well as of the colonies; that it is, and should be recognized as, the one and only road to unity of the Empire.

The key-note of Lord Durham's report and of the policy to which it gave rise, was constructiveness. Constructiveness has been characteristic of the British as of the Roman race, but the constructive genius of either race has shown itself in different ways. The Romans set themselves to build up one

Empire on a despotic model. To make the one whole, they kept the parts divided, in order to concentrate strength at head-quarters. The English for the last sixty or seventy years have set themselves to build up nations within the Empire. They have taken the method of devolution, and made the parts into larger units, thereby giving them greater strength relatively to the centre. The success in doing so up to the present date has been due to greater continuity in this respect than has always been apparent in British history overseas. It has been pointed out in a previous chapter that the Romans were far superior to the English in continuity of policy, and that want of continuity has been the chief failing of the English in the matter of their Empire. It is difficult to dissociate a Government from a people. The kind of people produces the kind of Government; and party Government in England, which is at the root of any want of continuity in policy, is the product of English love of freedom. But, so far as Government and people can be dissociated, want of continuity in British colonial policy has been due to the Government rather than to the people; and in giving freedom to the younger British communities of the Empire, and creating or encouraging larger units, there has for once been continuity of policy on the part of successive Governments, with the happiest results up to the present time. It may be summed up that the United Kingdom and the Self-Governing

Dominions have been held together up to the present time, because, apart from what may be called temporary sources of irritation, there has been no substantial reason why any of the Self-Governing Dominions should wish to part from the Mother Country and leave the Empire, and there have been substantial reasons why they should not want to leave it.

The dependencies of Great Britain, as opposed to the Self-Governing Dominions, like the Roman Provinces, have, speaking generally, been held by force, open or in reserve, but by force perpetually receding into the background as good government has produced good will. At the risk of vain repetition, the main features of the story of Great Britain and her dependencies, as opposed to the Self-Governing Dominions, may once more be summarized as follows.

Trade has bred conquest, and conquest has developed into rule. Similar stages can be traced in the overseas history of other European nations; but beyond the seas, as at home, in spite of much want of continuity of policy, and in spite of a mischievous characteristic of Englishmen at home to assume that the laws and institutions which are good for Englishmen in England must necessarily be good for all other races under all other conditions, there has been more growth and evolution in British history than in the history of any other power with which Great Britain might be compared.

There has been much going backwards and forwards, greatly to the detriment of the subject races as well as of the dominant people, but on the whole there have been few violent breaks in the history, just as there have been few eras of meteoric brilliancy. The English did not overrun a world or a continent as the Spaniards overran Central and South America; nor did they rise from being traders to be conquerors and then sink back again. By holding their own, they gathered round them more than had been their own, and in every quarter of the world where the English have gone, there has been, over and above their great contests with other European nations, a gradual widening of the British sphere either by a series of small wars or by more peaceful means.

It has already been noticed that to the work of ruling the dependencies so acquired the British character has not brought any special power of assimilation. British citizens who have gone among coloured races have lived more outside them than has been the case, for instance, in the dependencies of the Latin peoples. This has been a source of strength rather than of weakness, not only on the assumption that the sphere of rule is to remain a sphere of rule, but probably also if the ideal of the future is that the sphere of rule is eventually to broaden out into something more than a collection of subject dependencies; for it must be counted as a gain that there is no apparent likelihood of self-

governing communities coming into being on any
great scale in the British Empire of the type to be
found in certain parts of Spanish America, where
hybrid populations handle democratic machinery
with little result beyond constant revolutions.
What the British character has contributed to the
task of ruling is honesty, as men go, and the instinct
of fair play, common sense, and practical constructiveness. The success which Great Britain
has attained in dealing with her dependencies has
been mainly due to the combination of the strong
hand with honesty and justice. She has given to
them from without what they had never received
from within, security for life and property, justice
between man and man, immunity from extortion,
law instead of caprice. Common sense has made
against violent changes, so that the English, like
the Romans, have on the whole dealt gently with
and turned to good account native customs and
institutions; and British constructiveness, as shown
in public works, has brought before the eyes of the
ruled unmistakable evidence that they have derived
material advantage from the rulers. The ruling
faculty is in fact the highest phase of constructiveness. The trader evolves into the ruler because the
making instinct in certain races is not satisfied by
merely making money.

Lastly, it will be noted that in the sphere of rule,
as in the sphere of settlement, this instinct or quality
of constructiveness is promoting larger units. If we

look at the Far East, we find the British dependencies in the Malay regions, including Borneo, more and more being grouped round or linked to a common centre at Singapore. If we turn to the West Indies, we find a growing tendency to some form of federation. If we take the case of West Africa, we find that all the Niger Territories and Lagos have lately been consolidated under one Government.

So far for the two halves of the Empire taken separately up to date. One half has been held to Great Britain as being the Mother Country, the other half has been held to Great Britain as being the ruling country; and, inasmuch as the two halves have remained mainly, though not wholly, aloof from each other, the link of Great Britain has kept the Empire one. But in turning from the past and present to try and decipher the future, we are met on the threshold with the forces of science and the fact that under our eyes they are changing and modifying our Empire. It is idle to speculate as to when distance will become a negligeable quantity, or whether and to what extent medical skill will transform the sphere of rule into a sphere of settlement, but one thing is certain, and that is that the two halves are for good or ill coming into constantly closer relations with each other. It will be well to consider the future, as we have reviewed the past, with respect to each half separately; but it must be borne in mind as regards the future, that the problem may be not whether the Self-Governing Dominions will remain with the United Kingdom, *quâ* the United Kingdom, but whether they will remain with the United Kingdom plus her dependencies. In other words, it is conceivable, though most unlikely, that England might at some future date have to choose between her sphere of settlement and her sphere of rule. This point will be further noticed below.

Taking the sphere of rule first, how will it be retained? The answer is fairly simple. As far as can be judged, it will be held simply and solely by the same means that have been hitherto employed, by good government with the strong hand behind it. It must, at the same time, be recognized, that being held on these lines and by these methods, the dependencies have been, or are being, more or less transformed. Good government and constructive work has meant not merely multiplying numbers by giving security for life and facilities for living, but also raising the status of peasantry or tribesmen, who before the advent of British rule were held of little or no account, linking up tribes and States and principalities into larger units, intellectual and moral development, and the partial substitution of British civilization for other civilizations or for many types of barbarism. As in the sphere of settlement, so in the sphere of rule, the policy of Great Britain has been the reverse of the *Divide et Impera* policy; but whereas in the sphere of settlement British methods have resulted mainly in broadening and enlarging without transforming, in the sphere of rule they are resulting to some extent in making something different in kind. New conditions, bringing in their train new problems, are being evolved to a greater degree in the sphere of rule than in the sphere of settlement, and science is setting itself to modify the effects of climate. Still, as has been pointed out in the last chapter with regard to India, the greatest British dependency, we have to look very far ahead to contemplate seriously a time when the dependencies of Great Britain will cease to be in the true sense dependencies ; and it may be safely concluded that if the British Empire simply consisted of Great Britain and her dependencies, it would be held together as long as, and no longer than, Great Britain retains her strength.

When we turn to the Self-Governing Dominions, there is no such simple answer to be given. There are two preliminary comments to be made, sufficiently obvious but not always sufficiently regarded. Aristotle has told us that the objects of revolutions are great but the causes or occasions of them are small.[1] It is these apparently small causes or occasions, originating with individuals rather than with Governments, which are most likely to make or mar the Empire. The individual had more to do than Government with making our Empire, and the individual will probably in the long run have more to do with keeping it. It is not statesmen who are

[1] Οὐ περὶ μικρῶν ἀλλ' ἐκ μικρῶν, *Politics* v. 4. 1.

going to have the final say as to whether the British families are going to come closer to one another or to drift further apart. The ultimate decision will rest with the men and women who make up the different British families, who live everyday lives, and are guided not so much by high State policy as by instinct and common sense. It is, therefore, a very great and real mistake to regard the future of the Empire as depending in the main upon Ministers and Government offices. It depends in an increasing degree, as distance diminishes and knowledge grows, upon the individual citizens.

It is also a great mistake to argue in regard to the problem of Empire as though men and women, and communities which are made up of men and women, did not act, as they do almost invariably act, from mixed motives; to lay down that sentiment is the one bond of Empire, or that the Empire wholly depends upon commercial interests, and so forth. What holds the Empire together and what will hold it, if it is held, is an aggregate of considerations, one of which will perhaps be predominant at one time and in one community and another in another, but none of which will hold the field exclusively.

Now, having seen how the Dominions and the Mother Country have so far been held together, let us ask what motives are there likely to be in the Dominions for separation from the Empire and what motives for remaining in it. The main motives for separation will be twofold, one more sentimental than practical, the other purely practical. The first will be the increasing and perfectly natural desire, which grown up peoples feel as strongly as grown up men, not to be subordinate even in name, to control their external as well as their internal relations, to be sovereign peoples in the eyes of the world. The second and practical motive is, or may be, the desire not necessarily to be involved in all the liabilities of the Mother Country, partly on financial grounds, partly from fear of in any way compromising existing autonomy. There have already been indications that a Dominion may not wish, when the Mother Country is at war with another power, necessarily to take an active part in the war, unless the war is to some extent of its own making and on its own behalf. Similarly, in the early days of the old American colonies, the New Englanders tried to make a treaty with Canada on the terms that they should remain at peace even though England and France were at war. With regard to this second motive, however, it is specially important to bear in mind the point which has already been emphasized, that the Self-Governing Dominions must not be treated or thought of as one in their relation to the Mother Country. Nor must it be forgotten that party Government holds the field in each of these Dominions as at home, and that, therefore, the views of one Government even on Imperial questions may be utterly different from those of another. The dominant feeling in one

Dominion at a given time may be to stand outside the liabilities of the Mother Country, and in another not to stand outside them so much as to have a voice in determining them. It is perhaps roughly true to say that the first of the two motives given above, the sentimental dislike of the appearance of subordination, operates, or is likely to operate, quite as strongly in the more purely British communities as in the more mixed communities; but that in the case of the second motive, if we allow for party government and the divergent views of Liberal, Conservative, and Labour parties, and try to strike an average, the more purely British communities are likely to be less desirous to stand outside the liabilities of the Mother Country and more desirous of full responsibility and partnership than the mixed communities. Where there is a strong French Canadian element or a strong American element as in Canada, or a strong Dutch element as in South Africa, there must naturally be, in a section of the population, a tendency to aloofness from liabilities which do not directly concern the particular Dominion.

Taking the other side of the account—the motives for remaining within the Empire—it may fairly be said that, even leaving out of sight the present undoubted value of the British connexion, communities, like individuals, however democratic, have a strong strain of Conservatism in them, and, unless some very special occasion arises or some very obvious gain is in view, they are slow to break entirely with the old order. Moreover, special occasions which make for union are as likely to present themselves as special occasions which make for division. At the present time, for instance, the foreign competition which threatens England's sea power is a strong stimulus to Imperial unity. Gratitude and good feeling again have weight in collections of men as in each individual man, and the British record towards the Self-Governing Dominions of the Crown is a bright record, which cannot be matched in history, of liberal and generous policy. The call of the race is strong, wherever the citizens are of British descent, and the mere sense of established nationhood in the Dominions may, and probably will, in a manner to be referred to later, make for the permanent continuance of the Empire.

If we balance these two sets of motives against each other, the path of salvation obviously lies in a continuance of the constructive policy of which Lord Durham was the pioneer, and which has so far proved successful. There is no other alternative; we have gone too far in one direction to think of turning back; we have created nations, and cannot uncreate them. We can only recognize and welcome existing conditions and move forward again.

It has been said that the Romans and the English have shown in a marked degree constructive genius; that the Romans, on the one hand, while giving much scope to municipal life in the separate provinces, were always intent on strengthening the centre, while the English, on the other hand, have applied themselves to building up the parts. Possibly it might be difficult to maintain that the constructive genius of the English has been actually greater than that of some other modern peoples, of the French, for example; but, at least, British constructiveness has had a character of its own. In creative work the British instinct has shown itself in the absence of a hard and fast system; in the rejection of schemes involving all or none; in the ready accep-tance of compromise; and in favouring evolution, growth, and development as opposed to complete novelty. British history tells us that whatever has been permanent in the work of the English has been the result of evolution from the past, not of breaking with the past, and that the English have built well because the builders have accommodated themselves to the times and the places and have not been hampered by elaborate plans, designs, and surveys drawn out beforehand by the Government.

In considering the future of the Empire it appears feeble and inconclusive not to sketch out a definite programme and to prescribe new machinery. Con-sequently we have a plethora of plans and schemes. But it is in the very attractiveness of schemes and programmes that the danger for the future consists. The British present has grown up on no definite plan. So far from being logical, it is a unity of contradictions, absolutely impossible on paper, but working very comfortably in fact. To anything like an orderly ground-plan of the future, British instinct, which constitutes British genius, is opposed. It is equally opposed to the all or none element, the absence of compromise which all schemes and plans usually imply. Clear and practical views are constantly obscured by the wholesale character with which both the supporters and the opponents of schemes invest them. There is only one sure guide to the future, and that is the race instinct which represents day to day opportunism.

What does continuance of a constructive policy mean? What is there left to construct? On the one hand, the process of strengthening the parts in relation to the centre can be carried on. Nationhood can be further encouraged among the young peoples of the Empire by constant recognition, as occasion offers—and occasion is constantly offering, the object being to eliminate as far as possible the first of the two motives for leaving the Empire, which is the sense and appearance of subordination. On the other hand, the future seems to call for some growing organization which will link the Mother Country and the Dominions each with each on terms of equality in lieu of the discarded terms of superiority and subordination. But this organization is well on its way in the form of the Imperial Conference, supplemented by subsidiary conferences for the discussion of single questions; while the calling

into being of a Standing Committee of Imperial
Defence presents obvious facilities for the development of Imperial co-operation. Nothing could be
more in harmony with the British instinct and
British methods of construction, than the evolution
of the Imperial Conference and its concomitants.
Twenty-five years have elapsed since the first meeting of the kind took place without any system of
any kind or any rule as to representation, and at the
present moment the Imperial Conference is a well-
defined, fully understood, and fully recognized
machinery, the meetings being held at stated
intervals, and each meeting resulting in a step
forward in the direction of Imperial unity. The
wonder is that it has developed so rapidly, not that
it has not developed further, and any attempt to
stimulate its growth by hothouse methods would be
disastrous. It would be disastrous, because it would
run counter at once to the British instinct and to
what has been described above as the second motive
for leaving the Empire, the dread of being involved
in external liabilities which would not be removed
at the present stage of development by having one
voice among several in the direction of a common
policy. The diversity between the Dominions, and
the operation of party Government in each Dominion,
makes for different views in regard to an Imperial
Council of one kind or another. It is, on this ground
alone, not only inexpedient but absolutely impossible
to build up the future except by slow degrees, if the

building is to endure. The more the parts are strengthened in relation to the centre, the more they recognize their strength, the less they will fear that autonomy will be injured by closer partnership.

When we turn from the question of political organization to that of commercial relations, we find the young peoples on the one side and the Mother Country so far on the other. Preference and Protection commend themselves to the young peoples, whereas the present generation in England has grown up under Free Trade. It is often suggested that the Dominions might under certain circumstances or for certain reasons wish to part with the Mother Country; but since we have outgrown the old Whig doctrines, there are few who suggest that England might wish to part with the Dominions. In fact it is probably true to say, though it may not be generally admitted, that as each succeeding year adds conspicuously to the population of the young peoples of the world, whether inside or outside the British Empire, the value of the Dominions to England increases in much greater proportion than the value of England to the Dominions, because each year each Dominion comes nearer the time when it can defend itself, and each year England, without the Dominions, tends to be more outdistanced in population and home resources by some of her foreign competitors. Nor does this statement exhaust the case. It is not merely a question of quantity, it is a question also of quality and of kind. The ascendancy of Europe in the world, of Old World methods and standards, is no longer unchallenged. The future is largely for the ' New Model ' among peoples, and in the competition of the future it is all-important for England to have by her side British peoples built, for better or worse, on the New Model.

From this it follows that if England is to hold her own as a nation, she must keep the Dominions with her ; and if she can only keep them with her by paying a price, the price must, if possible, be paid. Imperial Preference, therefore, cannot be regarded simply as an economic question. On the other hand, if the price is too high for the English to pay, they cannot and will not pay it, whatever may be the result, and may elect to part with the Dominions. But as the Dominions do not intend that the ties of Empire shall impede their own development, so they make no claim whatever that any step should be taken by England which should militate against the welfare of her people at home. The whole question is obscured by, and the whole danger to the future lies in the lust for a wholesale scheme and the desire of extreme Free Traders to saddle their opponents with a wholesale scheme. Again, the one and only safe guide is British instinct and readiness for practical compromise. It is not a case of all or none. Imperial Preference, as has already been said, is quite natural, more natural than Free Trade. Further, it is one of the many cases in which appearances are valuable. In the absence of any substantial preference being given, a definite indication of readiness to give preference to peoples within the Empire as against peoples without the Empire, so far as such preference will not be substantially detrimental to the Mother Country, would be of great effect. It is as necessary to reject the doctrine that to give better terms to our own peoples than to foreigners is unsound in principle, as to be cautious with regard to any novel and wholesale scheme. Imperial Preference is the goal to be aimed at. Little by little is the way to the goal.

British instinct, the instinct of wise opportunism, is the one and only safe guide to sound relations between the Self-Governing Dominions and the Mother Country. But we now come back to the point that the relations are not merely between the Self-Governing Dominions and the Mother Country, but between the Self-Governing Dominions (all different) on the one side, and on the other the Mother Country plus the dependencies. The possession by England of great tropical dependencies with multitudes of coloured British subjects already gravely complicates the relations between the Mother Country and the Self-Governing Dominions, and, as has been seen, is likely to complicate them still further, as coming and going increases, and makes the colour problem a continuously increasing difficulty. On the other hand, the existence of these British dependencies may, and probably will,

be found to supply the strongest of all motives
to the Self-Governing Dominions for remaining
within the circle of the British Empire. The
Self-Governing Dominions are respectively building up their national structures and their national
life, but the nearer they come to maturity and the
more they become conscious of having done their
necessary work at home, the more they are likely
to value partnership in a greater whole. It is a law
of nations, writ large in history, that when they have
completed the home edifice, rounded off the corners,
and given it final form and shape, the constructive
instinct seeks for new outlets beyond the seas. The
colonial Empires of European nations followed on
the achievement of national unity at home. Spain,
Portugal, Holland, France, Great Britain, all in
turn obeyed the law. United Italy has acquired
possessions in Africa, United Germany has felt
increasingly the call to colonial expansion and
Empire. Even the United States have not kept within
the limits to which they have applied the Monroe
doctrine, and that doctrine itself, in its latter-day
phases, is little less than a claim to a Protectorate
far beyond the actual boundaries of the great
Republic. The younger nations of the Empire are
not likely to be exceptions to the rule ; and if they,
too, must find an outlet in their turn, how can they
find it but by retaining their British citizenship and
entering into the heritage side by side with the
citizens at home ? Or even if they could find it

178 THE BRITISH INSTINCT

otherwise, what opening would be comparable in greatness and in worth to that which the British Empire offers ? The fact that under existing conditions the Self-Governing Dominions have such scope for future history, and that they would lose it were the present supremacy of the Motherland to be wrested from her by foreign rivals, may well, in an increasing degree, make the sentiment of kinship, which is patriotism for the Empire, coincide with a sense of common interests ; and to young peoples, who look to the future, the possibilities of sharing greatness are likely to appeal with more potency than any dread of incurring liabilities. Meanwhile every citizen from the sphere of settlement who serves the Empire in the sphere of rule is a missionary in the cause of holding the Empire together ; and the more openings that are found in the Imperial Services for the white sons of the Empire from beyond the seas, the greater will the number of such missionaries be, and the more it will be brought home to the younger peoples that it is worth while to stay in the British Empire.

INDEX

Oxford : Horace Hart, M.A., Printer to the University

For EU product safety concerns, contact us at Calle de José Abascal, 56–1°, 28003 Madrid, Spain or eugpsr@cambridge.org.

www.ingramcontent.com/pod-product-compliance
Ingram Content Group UK Ltd.
Pitfield, Milton Keynes, MK11 3LW, UK
UKHW012344130625
459647UK00009B/521